Current Good Practices and New Developments in Public Service Management

A Profile of the Public Service of the United Kingdom

Current Good Practices and New Developments in Public Service Management

A Profile of the Public Service of the United Kingdom

The Public Service Country Profile Series: No. 2

Commonwealth Secretariat
1995

The views expressed in this document do not necessarily reflect the opinion or policy of the Commonwealth Secretariat.

Printed and Published by the Comonwealth Secretariat

May be purchased from:
Commonwealth Secretariat Publications
Marlborough House
Pall Mall
LONDON SW1Y 5HX

ISBN: 0 85092 413 8

Price: £8.95

FOREWORD

Since 1975, the Commonwealth Secretariat, through its Management and Training Services Division, (formerly the Management Development Programme) has been providing extensive assistance to Commonwealth governments confronting the challenge of securing administrative and managerial improvements in the public sector. The Division's analyses of major trends and opportunities for public sector reform are complemented by its tailored consultancy and training packages designed in response to national and regional needs.

The current widespread debate concerning the managerial and structural options which will best fit the public service for the challenges of the next century touches the very centre of the questions concerning the role and responsibilities of the governments of the future.

The structure and processes of the overall public sector, that area of national social and economic life which is directly answerable to government, are significant in two ways. They serve to deliver, or to fail to deliver, the policy objectives of government, and they serve as a marker which government unavoidably sets down concerning accountability and transparency in national affairs, and the legal and constitutional framework for development.

As the range of structural options and accountability relationships utilised within the public sector increases, the complexity and diversity of that sector is growing. Assessing the strategic options for the public sector requires a clear understanding of the managerial alternatives and the actual and potential capacities of the core public service. I believe that this publication, and its companion volumes, is a significant contribution towards that understanding.

The Public Service Country Profile Series has grown out of a larger publication series examining current good practices and new developments in public service management. A pan-Commonwealth expert working group met in Kuala Lumpur in early 1993 to discuss the possible development of a policy guide for senior officials, highlighting the key principles underpinning recent managerial developments within the public service. This ground-breaking workshop developed the framework for *The Commonwealth Portfolio*, a distillation and analysis of innovations and best practices in public service management from across the Commonwealth.

The Commonwealth Portfolio is being published in loose-leaf format for easy updating, and its 65 entries will cover the major areas of change within public service management.

I am particularly pleased to note that in constructing the Portfolio the expert editors and compilers have been determined to ensure its relevance to the real challenges faced by senior officials and managers. To ensure that the principles it identifies are firmly grounded in real experiences and genuine achievements within the public service, member governments across the Commonwealth were approached to take part in a unique mapping exercise, identifying the actual changes which had been made in some key areas of public service management. That so many governments unhesitatingly agreed is a tribute to the spirit of co-operation and to the strength of professional networks within the public services of Commonwealth countries.

The Public Service Country Profile Series sets out the results of that mapping exercise, country by country, to provide an unprecedented insight into the real managerial and structural changes under way in the public service. In providing some firm ground on which those public servants, both elected and appointed, who are faced with the challenge of public service reform can stand while assessing the options available, the Country Profile Series marks a milestone in the debate concerning the management of the public service. Reality is informing rhetoric at last.

Dr Mohan Kaul
Director
Management and Training Services Division
Commonwealth Secretariat

ACKNOWLEDGEMENTS

This publication is the product of some remarkable co-operation and some very generous assistance from experts and officials at all levels who have given their time and knowledge as a contribution towards Commonwealth co-operation and as a signal of their commitment to the improvement of the public service.

I would very particularly like to thank David Askew of the U.K. Civil Service who undertook the initial detailed research and Marian Stuart who provided additional material and editing.

The Secretariat is very grateful to all those within the Civil Service who have found time to assist in this project. The publication owes a particular debt of gratitude to the Department of Trade and Industry and to the Recruitment and Assessment Services agency for agreeing to release David Askew and Marian Stuart respectively, and to the Cabinet Office for the very considerable assistance in establishing such productive co-operation.

Sir Kenneth Stowe provided most valuable suggestions in designing the publication series and concerning the style and content of all the country profiles.

The introduction was kindly provided by David Falcon.

The cover design was provided as a corporate contribution towards Commonwealth co-operation through the kind assistance of Francis Plowden of Coopers and Lybrand, London.

Roy Chalmers and Greg Covington have assisted immeasurably in all aspects of the production of this series.

The material in this publication was provided by many individuals and organisations, originally co-ordinated through David Askew and edited by Marian Stuart and myself. Although every attempt has been made to retain the accuracy of the contributing authors, final responsibility for any errors or inaccuracies rests clearly with the editors. The inclusion of any material does not imply that the contents have been approved or authorised by the U.K. Government.

Nick Manning
Adviser(Organisation Structure and Design)/*Project Co-ordinator*
Management and Training Services Division
Commonwealth Secretariat

CONTENTS

INTRODUCTION

Background

This introduction[1] describes the process of change that is taking place in the U.K. Civil Service, discusses the impact of the changes on the quality of the service received by the public and draws some conclusions about the conditions that appear to have been critical to the achievement of change.

The U.K. Civil Service contains over half a million people and is engaged in a very wide range of activities, from the direct delivery of services to members of the public to the provision of policy advice to Ministers on major affairs of state. Since the Northcote-Trevelyan reforms of the nineteenth century, the basic values that have underpinned the U.K. Civil Service are summarised in an ethical code set out by Peter Hennessy who identifies the following elements:

- probity;
- care for evidence;
- respect for reason;
- willingness to speak truth unto power;
- the capacity, not just to live with the consequence of what is conceived to be a mistaken course of action, but to pursue it energetically;
- awareness of other people's life chances;
- equity and fairness;
- constant and careful concern for the law;
- constant concern for Parliament – its needs and procedures; and
- concern for democracy.

There have been previous attempts to reform the Civil Service in the twentieth century, the most notable since the war being that proposed in the Report of the Fulton Committee. The underlying ethical code and dominant administrative culture survived all these attempts at reform. The administrative culture was essentially bureaucratic, driven by top-down directives and procedural control rather than performance objectives and devolved authority. The reforms of the 1980s and 1990s described in this paper have certainly changed the administrative culture to a managerial culture. Questions remain regarding the preservation of the ethical code within these changes, and the extent to which greater openness is necessary to provide new checks and balances to compensate for the loss of those inherent in the traditional administrative culture.

The Conservative Government of 1979 led by Margaret Thatcher sought to reduce public expenditure in order to reduce direct taxation in line with its overall economic policies. The view was taken that the U.K. was "over-governed" and that it would be in everyone's interests for government to play a smaller role. Simultaneously, the Government aimed to place in private ownership a number of public utilities, in order to subject them to direct market forces and so improve their efficiency and competitiveness.

The drive for economy and efficiency, and the contribution that greater competition could make to their achievement underlie much of the philosophy which started the Civil Service reforms. The importance of the Government's belief in privatisation as the root of other changes in public services should not be under-estimated. Coupled with a belief in the market, there was a belief that, freed from the intervention of politicians and bureaucrats, enterprises flourish and managers operate in ways that could be adopted with advantage by their counterparts in the public sector.

The Efficiency Unit and Scrutiny Exercises

An early manifestation of the desire to introduce private sector practice into those areas of government not appropriate for privatisation was the creation in 1979 of the Prime Minister's Efficiency Unit, led initially by Sir Derek Rayner, Chief Executive of Marks & Spencer. The Efficiency Unit has always been staffed by very able civil servants and people from the private sector on short term secondments. Typically the Unit has comprised two civil servants and three seconded industrialists, with a support staff of three.

The Unit developed a methodology based upon Scrutiny Exercises, working closely with civil servants from individual departments on narrowly focused and short term (typically 90 days) studies with the major aim being to reduce expenditure and improve the efficiency of the work of the department. About twenty scrutinies are conducted each year by government departments with support from the Unit. Some scrutinies cross the boundaries of a number of departments and on such occasions would be led by a member of the Unit.

The size of the Efficiency Unit is critical. It is not responsible for conducting scrutiny exercises; it is responsible for ensuring that scrutiny exercises are conducted. Placing the responsibility for the work firmly within the departments concerned has ensured a far greater involvement in the process and commitment to the outcome than would have been the case had the process been an external one.

A scrutiny works by examining closely a single activity or function. It sets out to establish what actually happens; provide facts and figures that are soundly based; challenge assumptions that hold back fresh thinking and better use of resources; demonstrate the necessary change can be brought about; and achieve measurable improvement within two years. Scrutinies are usually carried out within an individual government department. Terms of reference, action plan and implementation time-table are agreed with the Minister and the head of the department. Resulting report aims to present specific, fact driven recommendations with a time-table for action. After two years, the department produces an implementation report showing what has been achieved as a result. Scrutinies are a well proven way of focusing on action to exploit opportunities for real improvements. In recent years the Government claims they have produced savings and benefits valued at around £200 million to £300 million annually.

The early scrutinies revealed just how poor management was in the Civil Service and this is not at all surprising. Those identified with the potential to become future senior civil servants have not, traditionally, been recruited on the basis of their managerial capabilities or potential, though increasingly an attempt is made at the point of entry to assess their potential as managers. Prestige in the Civil Service has been associated with the preparation of policy advice and the provision of support to ministers. The routine business of executing the Government's policies and delivering services to the public carried less status. Traditional bureaucratic systems have always been dominated by the establishment and interpretation of rules; the process of impartially interpreting the rules was given greater emphasis than has concern with economy, efficiency and effectiveness and the quality of the outcomes achieved.

The Financial Management Initiative

The effect of the Efficiency Unit's activities was more widespread than the sum of the particular outcomes of the individual scrutiny exercises, as fundamental flaws in the Civil Service's approach to management were revealed. The Financial Management Initiative (FMI), introduced in 1982, was the next major step in developing managerial approaches.

The traditional approach to financial management in the Civil Service has been based on the detailed budget, establishing on an annual basis the funds provided for very specific heads of expenditure. The power to vire money from one budget head to another was severely restricted and good financial management equalled adherence to budget figures. Over-spending on particular budget heads would have to be explained in detail; under-spending was perceived to carry its own penalties as it would result in a reduction in the following year's budget allocation.

The aim of the FMI was to improve management in the Civil Service by ensuring that all managers knew what their objectives were and how their achievements would be assessed; that they had well defined responsibilities for making the best use of their resources and the necessary information, training and advice to exercise their responsibilities effectively.

As a result of FMI, managers in government departments were for the first time given responsibility for managing their own budgets. Output was measured and the cost-effectiveness of their work evaluated. Managers became personally accountable for their work as each department was required to operate within a limit for its manpower and total running costs. This approach has underpinned subsequent reforms. Key features were therefore:

- delegated budgets;
- the development of information systems; and
- increased objective setting, establishment of performance indicators and output measurement may the cost effectiveness of work to be evaluated.

The FMI was steered by the Treasury, which has a natural interest in promoting cost awareness, and reflected a preparedness among senior Treasury officials to loosen the powerful central controls that dominated Treasury approaches in the past. The success of the FMI has been attributed to its decentralisation of control and responsibility to line managers, and to its flexibility in allowing individual departments to tailor their own systems within a general framework.

The FMI has greatly accelerated the implementation of sophisticated, computer based accounting systems and the quality of information reaching Ministers and their senior civil servants has increased as its quantity has decreased.

The FMI also raised fundamental questions about personnel management practice in the Civil Service. Performance appraisal systems used to concentrate on the individual's performance in isolation – now the trend is towards schemes which are more concerned with assessing the extent to which an individual has contributed to the achievement of an organisation's goals in a particular period. But, in addition, managers need greater authority than they have had in the past to switch resources between staffing and non-staffing heads, to vary staffing grades and skills and to have greater freedom in hiring, firing, transferring, promoting and motivating staff.

The FMI was not conceived broadly enough to encompass such changes, nor was the Treasury prepared to permit them in a programme that was very much under its control.

The Next Steps Study

Sir Derek Rayner was succeeded in 1983 as Head of the Efficiency Unit by Sir Robin Ibbs, a former Director of ICI and subsequently Deputy Chairman of Lloyds Bank. Under him, the Unit was invited by the Prime Minister to conduct an investigation with the following terms of reference:

- to assess the progress achieved in improving management in the Civil Service;

- to identify which methods had been successful in changing attitudes and practices;

- to identify the institutional, administrative, attitudinal and political obstacles to better management and efficiency that still remain; and

- to report to the Prime Minister on what further measures should be taken.

The study, which took place between November 1986 and March 1987, involved the team in meeting Ministers, Permanent Secretaries and officials both inside and outside the Civil Service as well as some private sector organisations. The team visited dispersed units of central departments and regional offices and consulted people who had left the Civil Service for other work. Thus the study reflected a broad spectrum of opinion, which was important at the later implementation stage.

The report[2] was delivered to the Prime Minister in the spring of 1987, but the sensitivity of its recommendations and the forthcoming general election, meant that it was not published until February 1988.

The main findings of the study were:

- some progress had been made: civil servants were now more cost conscious, and management systems were in place;

- budgeting systems and manpower cuts were the two measures which had been most effective in changing attitudes and practices;

- while the introduction of systems was a start, real changes in attitudes and institutions were needed to get the full benefits of better management;

but substantial obstacles still remained:

- there was insufficient focus on the delivery of government services (as opposed to policy and ministerial support), even though 95 per cent of civil servants work in service delivery or executive functions;

- there was a shortage of management skills and of experience of working in service delivery functions among senior civil servants;

- short-term political priorities tended to squeeze out long-term planning;

- there was too much emphasis on spending money, and not enough on getting results; and

- the Civil Service was seen as being too big and too diverse to be managed as a single organisation.

The report was consistent with many of the findings of individual scrutiny exercises as well as echoing the recommendations of earlier reports, and in particular that of the Fulton Committee in 1968.

From their findings, the Unit team identified five main issues and three main priorities. The issues identified were:

- a lack of clear and accountable management responsibility, and the self-confidence that goes with it, particularly among the higher ranks in departments;

- the need for greater precision about the results expected of people and of organisations;

- the need to focus attention on outputs as well as inputs;

- the handicap of imposing a uniform system in an organisation of the size and diversity of the present Civil Service; and

- the need for sustained pressure for improvement.

The priorities identified were:

- the work of each department must be organised in a way that focuses on the job to be done; the systems and structures must enhance the effective delivery of policies and services;

- the management of each department must ensure that their staff have the relevant experience and skills needed to do the tasks that are essential to effective government; and

- there must be a real and sustained pressure on and within each department for continuous improvement in the value for money obtained in the delivery of policies and services.

The central recommendation of the report was that "Executive Agencies" should be established to carry out the executive functions of government within a policy and resources framework approved by the Minister responsible for that area of work. Each Agency should be under the direction of a Chief Executive who would have significant delegated authority within the policy and resources framework to manage the Agency and would be given freedom from the day to day involvement of Ministers.

Despite the controversy that was stimulated by the report, and the Treasury was clearly reluctant to free Agencies from areas of its direct control, the Prime Minister endorsed its findings on the report's publication in February 1988 and announced the first list of potential Agencies. The mechanism for planning and executing the reforms was also announced at this stage. A Project Manager, with the rank of Second Permanent Secretary, was appointed to lead a small team of civil servants. This team, known as the Next Steps Team, is responsible for identifying candidates for Agency status, for supporting the design of their Framework Documents and for encouraging the necessary management development and training. This clearly requires working very closely with individual departments as well as promoting the concept throughout the Civil Service and beyond. The team has subsequently played a central role in the process of evaluating the success of individual Agencies and reviewing their framework documents.

Political Commitment

The critical importance of ministerial leadership and support was recognised. The report stated:

> "Without this lead (the recommendations) will falter partly because of the inertia of any very large organisation, but partly because it is Ministers who will have to explain, promote and defend them in Parliament as and when the difficulties are encountered."

The Prime Minister continued to demonstrate a direct interest in the progress of the initiative and stated in the Civil Service management journal:

> "One of the great tasks we face for the 1990s is to improve our public services and make them more responsive to people's needs. Next Steps, which I launched two years ago, puts this to the top of the agenda. .... Next Steps sets the direction for the Civil Service of the future. The test will be improved results and better service. I am sure this is what we will see."

John Major, Prime Minister from November 1990, also signalled his support:

> "What we are seeing at the moment is nothing less than a revolution in Management in the Civil Service that will make it more responsive, more open, more effective, more rewarding for the clientele of the Civil Service's operations and I think providing a better career structure and a more enjoyable life for Civil Servants themselves."

Whilst political support and commitment from the very top has been of critical significance to the changes described in this paper, the political support needs to have a wider basis. This wider basis has come from consideration by the Treasury and Civil Service Committee (TCSC), one of the Select Committees of the House of Commons. TCSC has published a number of major reports on the Next Steps Initiative since 1988 and, by achieving a political consensus on each occasion, has demonstrated the importance of preserving the tradition of a politically neutral Civil Service whilst ensuring that the Civil Service is organised in such a way that it can efficiently and effectively implement the policy of the government of the day. At the time of writing (August 1994) a further report from TCSC is awaited and a more critical stance towards the reform programme is anticipated.

In a lecture delivered in May 1991 to the Royal Institute of Public Administration, the Shadow Chancellor of the Exchequer (Opposition Spokesman on Finance) recognised this:

"I do not think there would be merit in a new government seeking to uproot all the plants in the garden, re-arrange their roots, and then, having planted them again, expect them to grow well..... It is worth noticing that the framework agreement controlling an agency can be altered by government and one option for a government, which has different aims and values, is to change the agreement in line with its purposes."

This statement demonstrates that the reformed Civil Service is structured in such a way that it is possible for a new government to make substantial policy changes and reflect these changes in rewritten Framework Documents which would ensure rapid implementation of new policy measures.

Implementing the changes

Before any Agency is established a "prior options" study is carried out. This considers:

- whether the function needs to be carried out at all, if not it can be abolished;
- if the function does need to be carried out, whether it could be privatised or contracted out; and
- if it is to be a direct government function, whether it should be carried out by an Agency.

Each Agency has defined responsibilities, and clear aims and objectives, set out in a Ministerially-approved Framework Document. It operates within, and gives effect to, policies laid down by Ministers. It is set annual performance targets approved by its Ministers. The Chief Executive of the Agency is personally responsible for the Agency's performance in relation to these objectives and targets. The Agency's performance is monitored by its department, and full details of the tasks the Agency are given, and its performance against them, published in its Annual Report and Accounts. The Next Steps programme, in line with the Government's policy of openness, has resulted in a significant increase in the amount of information available to MPs and the public. The publication of agency Annual Reports and Accounts means that comprehensive information about the working of the Government machine is now readily available to anyone who wants it. This could previously have been obtained, if at all, only with considerable difficulty. This Review also ensures that the salient points about Agencies and their activities, including their performance against key targets, are brought together in a convenient form. Ministers, of course, retain unchanged accountability for policy, and answer to Parliament on it. Agency Chief Executives normally reply to letters from MPs or written Parliamentary questions about operational matters within their responsibility. This strengthens accountability, since those responsible for operational decisions are seen to be directly answerable for them.

The Next Steps approach, building on the Financial Management Initiative, links together more clearly aims and objectives, programmes and resources. Financial control has been strengthened and all agencies have clear financial targets. Making sure that Agencies have the right financial framework is essential. Twelve agencies are now operating as trading funds. This allows them to exercise considerable freedom and discretion in the management of their own funds. They are not subject to detailed advance approval by Parliament of their income and expenditure which could inhibit effective management of trading organisations, but are required to break even taking one year with another, and to meet any other targets Ministers may set, and are subject to many of the disciplines which apply to private sector companies. A number of other Agencies are considering trading fund status. Regardless of whether or not they can trade, Agencies are required to publish commercial-style accounts, on an accruals basis. If they are not able to do so when they are launched, the aim is that such accounts should be produced within two years of the launch. This is encouraging a more business-like approach and providing harder information from which agencies can work to improve efficiency.

Within this framework, a major impact of Next Steps has been to focus attention on unit costs. A growing number of Agencies have productivity targets based on unit cost information, and work is going forward with agencies to help ensure that the tools for measuring productivity are as effective as possible. This is essential if standards are to be maintained and improved at a time of public expenditure restraint and tight running-cost and paybill controls.

A key feature of Next Steps is the appointment of a Chief Executive, with freedom and flexibility to manage his or her operation. Chief Executives are normally appointed through open competition to get the best person – whether a civil servant or an outside appointee – for the job. Of the 98 Chief Executive and Chief Executive-designate appointments made so far, 65 have been recruited via open competition. Of those, 35 have come from outside the Civil Service, from a wide variety of backgrounds including the private sector, local government, the NHS, and the academic world. It is one of the objectives of the Next Steps Team that Chief Executives should have the managerial freedoms and flexibilities they need and that the disciplines to which they are subject should be related to the job to be done. The application of uniform Civil Service terms and conditions to such a diverse group of organisations is no longer appropriate. All Agencies have been encouraged to review their pay and grading arrangements and to consider devising their own pay and grading systems where this will lead to value for money.

By April 1994 nearly 350,000 civil servants, 60 per cent of the total were working in Agencies and other organisations operating on Next Steps lines. The programme includes all those areas of central government with which many people will most often deal such as the Inland Revenue, Customs and Excise, the Employment Service and the Benefits Agency, the Driver and Vehicle Licensing Authority and the U.K. Passport Office. Two new official bodies – the Child Support Agency and the Northern Ireland Child Support Agency – have been established from the outset as Agencies. Agencies range in size from the Social Security Benefits Agency with nearly 65,000 staff to Witton Park with only 30. Their work covers tasks as diverse as weather forecasting, managing prisons, issuing driving licenses and passports and providing support services to the Armed Forces. A further 94,000 civil servants work in areas announced as agency candidates and other areas are also under consideration. Existing Agencies and announced Agency candidates together account for 78 per cent of the total Home Civil Service. By the end of 1993 the principal areas of Home Civil Service activity (i.e. excluding the Northern Ireland Civil Service), which are potential Agency candidates had been identified. The aim is now to ensure that most of the candidates are up and running as agencies by mid 1995. (In Northern Ireland, because the Next Steps programme started later, the respective dates are end 1994 and mid 1996.)

One of the most important lessons to be drawn from this exercise is the part played by the centre of government. In other countries, the centre has sought to lay down an detailed blueprint to which all parts of the Civil Service have been expected to conform. Understandably, this has led to resistance from those subject to such direction. Elsewhere, the centre has established a number of strategic principles and has then encouraged individual units to adopt and adapt those that are relevant. Again, understandably, organisational inertia has meant that there has been limited change. In the U.K. a balance has been struck, with clear direction from the centre that change must occur within an overall framework, but considerable devolved authority to decide how best to interpret the principles in the context of the particular activity. The role the Next Steps Team has been to ensure that Agencies have been created, but the detailed work has been a matter for departments. This is also true for the management training and development that must be undertaken to ensure successful implementation. The Next Steps Team, and the Civil Service College are there to help, but each department must develop its own strategy and identify the appropriate sources of seminars, courses etc to meet its staff development needs.

The Civil Service College, itself an Executive Agency, has gone through a major change as a consequence of the reform programme. It no longer receives a centrally allocated budget but must cover all its costs from income earned from enrolling civil servants in its courses. This has led to much more careful market research into the real needs of senior civil servants. The Development Division in the Cabinet Office has encouraged good practice in staff development and every civil servant with a managerial role is appraised on the extent to which the staff for whom she or he is responsible have had their skills and knowledge developed, through attendance at training courses or otherwise.

Quality and the Citizens' Charter

Whilst the early stress in public sector reform has been on the twin concepts of *Economy* and *Efficiency*, a third and more fundamental concept, that of *Effectiveness*, has also become a matter for attention and the Government has paid increasing attention through the reform programme to the quality of the outcomes achieved by the Civil Service, reflecting the strong managerial emphasis underlying the reforms. The approach also reflects attempts to weaken "producer capture" of the public services in favour of the interest of the "customers", although considerable difficulties remain to be resolved in determining just who the customer is for many services, for example, the prison service.

The Executive Agency concept has many advantages for this approach. The Framework Document and Business Plans set out in a far more explicit way than previously just what each executive arm of the Civil Service exists to achieve. Ministers cannot hide behind ambiguous statements of purpose and civil servants cannot excuse the failure to deliver quality services on such ambiguity. Members of the public, citizens if not customers, have access, both directly and through their Members of Parliament, to such information and are, rightly, being encouraged to expect standards of service to achieve the target levels that have been set.

In July 1991 the Prime Minister launched the Citizens' Charter Initiative. This is a ten-year programme designed to raise the standards of public service. The Prime Minister has said:

> "The Citizens' Charter is changing the face of public services in the United Kingdom. It has a simple but ambitious aim: to raise the standard of public service up to and beyond the best of the present available and to make them answer better to the needs of ordinary people. It has six key principles – setting standards, information and openness, choice and consultation, courtesy and helpfulness, putting things right and value for money. These are being adopted throughout the Public Service.
>
> "The Charter Initiative embraces greater competition, independence scrutiny of public services; greater accountability and openness and a programme of management change to improve our public services. It ensures the needs and wishes of those who use these services come first."

The Citizens' Charter White Paper (CM1599) set out the principles to be followed in the public service and a comprehensive programme of specific improvements to those services. In April 1992 the Prime Minister appointed a Cabinet Minister with responsibility for carrying the programme forward.

The Charter is based on the recognition that much of the cost of public services is paid for by individual citizens, either directly or through their taxes. Citizens are entitled to expect high quality services, responsive to their needs, provided efficiently at a reasonable cost. Where the State is engaged in regulating, taxing or administering justice, these functions too must be carried out fairly, effectively and courteously. The approach aims to give more power to citizens. It is not a recipe for more state action, but a statement of a government's belief in the right of citizens to be informed and choose for themselves.

The Charter also recognises that those who work in the public sector are keen to improve the services that they provide and that they have the skills, dedication and enthusiasm to do so. What they have sometimes lack is the freedom and the encouragement to try out new ideas.

The Charter programme is being pursued in a number of ways and is not a blueprint which imposes a uniform pattern on every service. It is a tool kit of initiatives and ideas to raise standards in the way most appropriate to each service. There are four main themes to the Charter's strategy:

- Quality – a sustained new programme for improving the quality of public services;
- Choice – choice, wherever possible between competing providers;
- Standards – the citizen must be told what service standards are and what he/she can do if those standards are not met; and
- Value – the citizen is also a taxpayer; public services must give value for money within the total resources the nation can afford.

The Citizens' Charter meets the challenge of raising standards as well as increasing efficiency by focusing on results. The key is to look at the job to be done and then to work out how best to do it, applying a number of tests with the aim of introducing choice and competition wherever possible. This encourages public services to respond to their customers' needs, to reward innovation, and to improve the effectiveness and job satisfaction of staff. The key questions build on those used to establish whether an agency should be introduced:

- Does the job need to be done at all? – bureaucracies have an inherent tendency to grow. Unnecessary tasks should be cut out so that resources can be used where they are needed more or the costs to the taxpayer reduced.

- If the activity must be carried out, does the Government have to be responsible for it? The Government may judge that many activities that it has carried out over the years may be done better by the private sector.

- Where the Government needs to remain responsible for an activity, does the Government have to carry out the task itself? To find this out the task may be put out to competition, either between firms in the private sector, or by inviting both the public and private sectors to compete in a "market-test". The aim, either way, is better value for money. By December 1993, £1.1 billion of activities had been exposed to competition as part of the Government's competing for quality programme.

- Where the job must be carried out within Government, is the organisation properly structured and focused on the job to be done? Managers and staff must be freed from unnecessary rules and allow to find better ways of providing the services that meet the needs of the users. Higher and more rigorous quality of service targets are being set for government Agencies year on year.

Agencies are leaders in delivering the Citizens' Charter commitment to customer service. Agencies which serve the public directly are now expected to publish Charters or Charter Standard Statements which describe how the Agencies will treat its customers and the standards of service that individual customers can expect. Agencies' commitment to high quality service means that performance targets and Charter Standards are aligned and give staff a clear message about what they are to achieve, with performance monitoring systems which cover both. When a new Agency is being set up, it will be expected to think about the service standards it will offer at the same time as it is preparing its framework document and planning documents so that a Charter or Standard Charter Statement can be published on launch. These documents will be expected to reflect an emphasis on building a strong customer focus into the Agency's thinking from the outset.

Competing for Quality

The reforms of the 1980s were aimed – step by step – at getting public service delivery system right. They reflected the Government's belief that a competitive market is the most efficient and responsive mechanism for providing goods and services. As the Citizens' Charter makes clear, one way to achieve increased choice is to bring private sector disciplines to bear on the way public services are run. Privatisation has therefore been a key strategy applied by the Government wherever possible. Regulatory bodies have been created where the public interest requires protection because of the remaining elements of monopoly.

An increasing range of services have been purchased from the private sector. In November 1991 the Government's White Paper "Competing for Quality" set out proposals for extending competition in the provision of services in both Central Government and the National Health Service. In Central Government, all departments and Agencies were set targets for work to be market-tested. The 1992-93 target amounts to a fifty-fold increase over previous targets for market-testing. The new areas to be tested covered a wide range of activities moving from traditional support services such as catering and cleaning to areas closer to the heart of government.

The Government claimed that there was no presumption that these activities would be contracted out to private suppliers. However, unless the private sector has a clear expectation of winning a significant amount of work, it can hardly be expected to invest the necessary resources in making bids. The Government claims a belief that the best in public services can match anything in the private sector and the objective is to promote fair competition so that the public services can achieve, everywhere, the best value for money for the customer and for taxpayer. Understandably, civil servants faced with, as they saw it, competing for their own jobs, were less than convinced.

The Future Shape of the Civil Service

In the five or six years since its launch, the Next Steps programme has transformed the organisation and working methods of the Civil Service. There is a continuing, dynamic process under way covering much of the Civil Service addressing:

- the scope for change in areas of departments not yet in Agencies: this includes looking at streamlining central financial, personnel, and headquarters support function as responsibilities and tasks are delegated to Agencies; addressing the scope for contracting out in market-testing of headquarters functions; and initiating "prior options" analysis of the case for Agencies status for those remaining executive functions;

- for Agencies, the change programmes described above plus the requirement to contribute to the government's contracting out/market-testing programmes; and

- for Agencies, the periodic review of status.

Agencies have announced candidates for Agency status in the Home Civil Service which represent 78 per cent of the total staff employed. Because each candidate for privatisation, contracting out or market-testing is judged on its merit, it is not possible to predict the precise size of the Civil Service by the mid 1990s. It is, however, clear that following Next Steps and other initiatives, it will be smaller and can figure on the following lines:

- central departments focused on strategic issues, resource allocation and facilitating best practice;
- centres of departments which are smaller, concentrating on policy-making, essential finance and personnel functions and the procurement of services from agencies all on contract; and
- Agencies with considerable management freedom operating within the framework of the Citizens' Charter.

In July 1994 the Government published a White Paper[3] setting out its policies on the civil service. After speculation about a radical step towards privatising all but a few key functions, the White Paper will be seen as a conservative document. The key changes of the past few years – achieving economy and efficiency, placing greater emphasis on standards of service, introducing basic management approaches with an emphasis on delegated authority and more explicit accountability – are all to be sustained. The Government's continued commitment to sustaining the key principles on which the Civil Service is based (integrity, political impartiality, objectivity, selection and promotion on merit and accountability through Ministers to Parliament) is stated. There is an implicit recognition that the market-testing initiative as a centrally imposed directive has failed as, in future, departments and Agencies will decide for themselves the extent to which the approach will help them achieve their twin targets of remaining within centrally determined running cost limits whilst achieving negotiated performance targets. The importance of the negotiation process in target-setting is recognised in order that staff at all levels have a sense of ownership of the targets. The White Paper demonstrates the Government's realisation that an over emphasis on reducing staff numbers can be counterproductive in terms of cost reductions. The lessons of contracting out work to former civil servants at consultancy fee rates have finally been learnt.

The greatest innovation in the White Paper is the proposal to create a "Senior Civil Service" for the (approximately 3,500) most senior staff in grades 1-5. The purpose of the proposal is to ensure the availability of a core of senior professionals of the highest calibre to support Ministers in policy formulation and implementation. Whilst most of these people will still follow a career in the Civil Service, open recruitment will be introduced so that new blood can be recruited at senior levels. Career and succession planning are to be sharpened so that the very able can see their route to the top, providing that their performance matches their promise. The concept of the "faststream", which appeared to label future leaders from the moment of selection, is to go. Staff in the Senior Civil Service are to have explicit contracts of employment, but the wholesale use of short-term and rolling contracts is not to be adopted. Contracts will be clear about periods of notice in different circumstances and the grounds on which employment can be terminated are to be set out in the contracts.

The White Paper discusses the role of the Civil Service Commissioners, the Head of the Home Civil Service and, in the case of Grade 1, 1A and 2 posts, the Prime Minister, in the process of appointment but is silent about the procedures for termination. The protection of a politically neutral Civil Service is not achieved merely through increasingly transparent appointment procedures. The Civil Service Commissioners are increasingly seen as the monitors of good recruitment and selection practice rather than the people directly responsible for those activities. This is fully in keeping with good management practice which delegates as much personnel management responsibility as possible down the line.

Although the White Paper states commitment to the basic principles of integrity and independence it is silent on additional measures to safeguard these principles, other than the recognition that the Treasury and Civil Service Committee is examining the case for a Civil Service Act and other mechanisms to protect standards of conduct and propriety. Those familiar with the Public Accounts Committee's report[4] on this issue would feel this to reflect undue complacency, whilst those who call for greater access to official information will not be satisfied with the statement that "Public disclosure and quotation of advice risks eroding the non-political nature of the Civil Service and the confidential relations between Ministers and Civil Servants."

Conclusions

The reforms described here are important in the U.K. As solutions to a particular set of problems in a particular context they are unlikely to be easily transplanted as solutions to other problems in other contexts. So, it is important to look beyond the product of the reforms, in this case Executive Agencies, to the process that resulted in the changes and consider whether there are lessons to be learnt from that process that are of relevance elsewhere.

The conditions suggested here as critical for the success of the change programme in the U.K. are:

- sustained political commitment to change on the part of the Government and a degree of cross-party agreement on basic principles;
- pressure to secure the most efficient use of resources;
- pressure to reduce the number of people in the Civil Service;

- opportunities for civil servants to participate in analysing the problems that are faced;
- responsibility for implementation being firmly placed with those responsible for sustaining the changes; and
- programmes of staff development linked directly to the reform programme.

The importance of political commitment from the Government and the degree of cross-party support that has been achieved have been discussed in this paper. The political independence and neutrality of the U.K. Civil Service is longstanding and generally regarded to be of great significance to the achievement of the effective management of the business of government. This is not the case in every country and the extent to which the senior ranks of the Civil Service in a country reflects the political interests of the governing party affects the extent to which consensus for reform can be achieved.

The external pressure from the International Monetary Fund (IMF) in the late 1970s and the internal pressure from Conservative Governments to reduce public expenditure through the 1980s created a climate in which priorities had to be examined much more carefully and the need to address the outcomes achieved was emphasised. This climate has been very supportive to the introduction of managerial concepts as they provide a framework to handle the choice of priorities in a structured fashion. It is unlikely that the progress made in the early 1980s in facing up to inadequate management systems would have been as rapid if there had not been these severe pressures to reduce both expenditure and staffing levels. Whilst many countries face the same external pressures in terms of their relationships with the IMF and World Bank, the political consequences of generating and sustaining the internal pressures need careful consideration.

The Ibbs Report of 1988 was written after much discussion with civil servants. Its analysis and proposals were therefore clearly recognised as accurate and welcomed by a far greater number of civil servants than had been the case twenty years earlier when the Fulton report was published. The importance of the process of consulting and gathering ideas from a wide range of civil servants is stressed if their commitment to implementation is to be achieved. This is the first major lesson to draw from the U.K. experience.

Three key organisational units can be identified in the change process: the Efficiency Unit, the Next Steps Team and the Charter Unit. All three units are very small in relation to the scale of the tasks they have addressed. The Efficiency Unit has not been responsible for conducting efficiency scrutinies – it has been responsible for ensuring that the efficiency scrutinies have been conducted. The Next Steps Team has not been responsible for setting up Executive Agencies – it has been responsible for ensuring that Executive Agencies have been established. The three units have been seen to have the direct support of the Prime Minister. This has been a powerful factor in helping fulfil their responsibilities. But, the great bulk of the work has been undertaken within departments, by people who were not only involved in managing change but knew that subsequently they would be involved in managing the changed arrangements. This is the second major lesson to draw from the U.K. experience – external forces are needed to effect change – internal forces have to be generated and harnessed to ensure that the changes are sustained.

The third major lesson to draw is a simple one – it is not possible to develop organisations without developing the people who work in those organisations. The analysis of training needs should flow directly from the organisational change process, identifying the skills that are needed and the extent to which the current management staff lack those skills. This leads directly to staff development programmes which can involve courses and seminars as well as learning from on-the-job experience.

It should come as no surprise that the three general lessons from the U.K. experience all relate to people, their involvement in analysing the problems, in determining and implementing the solutions and in developing their own skills to cope with the additional responsibilities.

Administrative reform must be about structures and management systems – the form of those structures and systems will depend very much upon the particular circumstances in any country. The effective development and maintenance of structures and systems depends upon people – that is true in any country.

David Falcon
London, August 1994

---

1. An earlier version of this paper was prepared for the Commonwealth Secretariat's Round Table on the Changing Role of Government Administrative Structures and Reforms held in February in Sydney, Australia, entitled "Civil Service Reform in the U.K.: A Case Study by David Falcon

2. Improving Management in Government: The Next Steps, HMSO 1988

3. The Civil Service: Continuity and Change CMND 2627 HMSO (Note: in the U.K. a White Paper is a statement of government policy whilst a Green Paper is a consultative document published during the stage of policy development. Unusually, the Government has invited comments on this White Paper)

4. Committee of Public Accounts (1994) The Proper Conduct of Public Business Eighth Report HMSO

SECTION 1: MAKING THE MOST OF STAFF

1.1 Ensuring non-discrimination in employment practices

1.2 Enhancing staff training and development

1.3 Improving human resource management, including performance management and performance appraisal

1.4 Performance incentives in the public sector, including delegated pay bargaining

1.5 Mission orientation

1.6 Recruitment and retention

1.7 Anti-corruption measures

1.8 Developing a Public Service Code of Conduct

1.9 Contractual employment

1.10 Workforce size control

1.11 Redundancy management

1.12 Human resource information systems

1.1 Ensuring non-discrimination in employment practices

This entry covers all types of discrimination – by gender, race, disability, and community background.

Gender and Race: The U.K. has a Programme for Action to achieve equality of opportunity for women and for people of ethnic minority origin in the Civil Service. The programme aims to help the Service to recruit, retain and promote the best available people, regardless of gender, marital status, domestic responsibilities, race or colour. It enables the best possible use of the abilities of all staff through career development, training and the operation of flexible working practices.

Disability: The U.K. Civil Service is committed to ensuring that there is no discrimination on the grounds of disability and that access to employment and advancement in the Civil Service is based on ability, qualifications and suitability for the work. There is currently a code of practice for this and the Office of Public Service and Science (OPSS) is preparing a Programme for Action on disability to complement the programmes on gender and race.

Community background: This applies in Northern Ireland only, not in the rest of the United Kingdom. A policy statement on religious equality of opportunity and a code of practice on monitoring reaffirm the commitment of the Civil Service to equality of opportunity for members of both the Protestant and Catholic communities. This operates in the framework of the law which protects individuals from unfair discrimination on the grounds of their religious affiliation or political opinion, and requires employers to ensure that their employment practices are fair.

The context for change

Gender: The Sex Discrimination Act 1975 (SDA) as amended makes direct and indirect discrimination between men and women in employment unlawful, except in very limited circumstances. It also makes it unlawful to discriminate against people who are married. It applies to government departments and Agencies as to any other employer. In addition, the Equal Pay Act 1970 as amended applies to government departments and agencies as to other employers, although the Civil Service has for many years had an equal pay policy. Government departments and agencies are expected to comply with the Code of Practice of the Equal Opportunities Commission. This provides guidance on the equal opportunity responsibilities of employers, individual employees, trades unions and employment agencies. The SDA also makes it unlawful to victimise an individual for making a complaint about discrimination or for giving evidence about such a complaint.

The objectives of U.K. Government policy in this field include:

- an equal opportunity strategy to operate in every department;
- regular reviews to ensure that issues of most relevance are being given appropriate priority;
- regular review of resources allocated to the work to ensure implementation of the programme;
- all managers and staff to be made aware of their responsibilities and rights in this field.

Race: The aim is to ensure that all staff have equality of opportunity to benefit from employment, training and advancement appropriate to their abilities, and to enjoy a working environment free from discrimination and harassment. There are statutory provisions in the Race Relations Act 1976.

The objectives are again to develop an equal opportunity strategy in all departments. Staff have been made responsible for implementing the policy and are accountable for doing so. There should also be regular reviews of progress and the resources allocated to the work.

Disability: Disabled people possess the same range of skills and abilities as non-disabled people. Furthermore, most people with disabilities are fully effective employees without special help. Many others have as much to offer as non-disabled people, given the help and equipment which is readily available. Among the objectives of the Code of Practice are:

- the development of a departmental strategy for implementing the Code;
- monitoring the effectiveness of policies in each department;
- making available advice to senior management, personnel managers and staff on disability matters;
- publicising disability policies and good employment practice to all staff;
- encouraging departments to liaise with the Disablement Advisory Service and other specialist organisations;
- promoting the availability of advice and guidance on disability in individual cases;

- requiring that a record is made of all staff who are registered under the Disabled Persons (Employment) Act 1944.

Community Background (Northern Ireland): The 1976 Fair Employment Act made direct discrimination on the grounds of religious belief or political opinion unlawful in the field of employment. A Fair Employment Commission has extensive powers to promote both equality of opportunity and affirmative action and to work to eliminate discrimination. It monitors the situation carefully, requiring a return showing the religious composition of the workforce and of applicants for employment. The Government was already well advanced in this field, and had for some time been monitoring whether the Civil Service was providing equal opportunities to both sections of the community in Northern Ireland. This led to the establishment of a Code of Practice.

The objectives are that each department and agency should monitor its own staff in accordance with the Code of Practice. They will also examine their own employment practices on a regular basis, using monitoring and labour availability statistics to check whether equality of opportunity appears to be being enjoyed by members of both communities in respect of recruitment, training and promotion.

Implementing change

Requirements for implementation of a programme to ensure non-discrimination are:

- a framework of anti-discrimination employment law, on which the public service as an employer can build its own policy;

- a network of administrative staff to collect data on the workforce, so that the extent of employment of any group (e.g. by gender, race or disability) can be measured;

- the enforcement of service-wide personnel procedures.

The U.K. has the various Acts of Parliament specified above and personnel units in each public service body who collect data on the gender, ethnic origin and disabilities of all staff, and teams in central departments who check, collate and publish the information. There are also rules issued by the Minister for the Civil Service about recruitment and advice from HM Treasury.

Key stakeholders include middle managers, because they have the most day-to-day effect on personnel practice. It is necessary to train them and to raise their awareness of non-discrimination practices. Permanent Secretaries of each Civil

Service department need to show commitment to the policy in order to motivate and convince staff at all levels in their department.

As far as costs are concerned, the Equal Opportunities Division of the Office of Public Service and Science in the U.K. has about 15 staff in post and an annual budget of about £600,000. The costs of non-discrimination in public service employment practices in the U.K. are not generally separated from the overhead cost of general personnel management.

On gender and race, progress reports show some demonstrable progress has been made in the several years that the programmes have been running. There is a target of fifteen per cent by the year 2000 for the number of women promoted on merit to the top three Civil Service grades. As far as race is concerned, a timescale was set for achieving a ninety per cent coverage in monitoring the workforce. It has taken several years to reach eighty two per cent and could take a few more to reach the ninety per cent target.

The recent White Paper "The Civil Service: Continuity and Change" affirmed the need to improve the representation of women, ethnic minority staff and disabled staff in senior positions. It announced that an Advisory Panel is being appointed to advise the Head of the Home Civil Service on the steps to be taken to improve representation in senior management positions of people from an ethnic minority background and people with disabilities.

Supporting material

(i) Equal Opportunities for Women in the Civil Service, Progress Report 1992-93, ISBN 0-11-430094-1, £4.50, 1993

(ii) Equal Opportunities in the Civil Service for People of Ethnic Minority Origin, Progress Report 1992-93, ISBN 0-11-430090-9, £5.75, 1993

(iii) The Civil Service: Continuity and Change, Cm 2627 HMSO, ISBN 0-10-126272-8, £7.10

1.2 Enhancing staff training and development

At the last count (1989/90) the U.K. Civil Service spent around £400 million on training during the year. Most training and development takes place within organisations and some is supplied by the Civil Service College, which now operates as a government agency and provides a wide variety of training courses for staff. Departments are free to spend their training budgets in any way they wish, and can and do often use external suppliers and consultants for training purposes.

Training itself should always be seen as a means to an end, rather than end in itself. Plans for training must therefore always stem from the needs of the business and be measured by the increased business performance that they have brought about. Much of the current activity in the public sector in the training and development area concentrates on how to identify the training need and measure the effect. It is less on the content of training or the method of delivery, which is already quite well understood.

The context for change

Government organisations in the U.K. are becoming increasingly oriented towards achieving results and so, particularly in Agencies, much effort is devoted to developing business skills. Even in traditional policy areas, the disciplines of the Financial Management Initiative and Market-Testing are altering the face of the Civil Service – and hence the training required for staff. In the U.K. there is if anything an over-abundance of training available in most disciplines and one of the difficulties is choosing the best from a selection of training suppliers.

In order to maintain and improve the service to Ministers and the management and delivery of public services whilst further improving efficiency, the Civil Service needs:

- to continue to develop a managerial, performance-based approach;

- to make better use of its most important resource – the staff of departments and Agencies – by providing the prospects of a career with a good employer; by developing their managerial and technical skills and by ensuring equality of opportunity for all members of staff, irrespective of backgrounds, gender, race and disability.

Implementing change

As a result of the fundamental reforms described in the Introduction, the centres of departments have delegated more and more discretion for action and responsibility for results to operational managers. Responsibility for training and development has followed a similar path. This has led to a much greater diversity of training needs, and training solutions to those needs.

There is also a growing awareness that government organisations, like any others, can only achieve success through their people, and that particularly in times of change an even greater flexibility is required in terms of the skills, knowledge and attributes that an individual contributes. This has tended to raise the status of the training and development function in organisations.

Departments and Agencies discharge their responsibility for the training and development of staff in different ways. The best approaches are characterised by:

- a firm grounding in the tasks of the organisation – both strategic and operational;

- acceptance that good staff development involves more than just good training courses. It includes on-the-job development, job moves and other opportunities to widen experience. it is planned through a close partnership between individuals, their line managers and the relevant specialist functions; and

- high quality training.

Training is obtained from a wide variety of sources, often including tailor-made programmes or individual courses designed either in-house or provided by external suppliers. In recent years, such training has focused much more clearly on the changing skills needed, including those of customer service.

Much is being done across the Civil Service to ensure that civil servants are equipped with the skills, experience and capabilities they need now and in the future. Many departments and Agencies have formal management development programmes in place at various levels. In particular these programmes are playing an increasingly important part in the development of staff with potential for early promotion. External qualifications feature in a number of the programmes.

There are important external standards which can help organisations adapt to the new climate of change, in particular "Investors in People" and National Vocational Qualifications.

All government departments are now carrying forward their plans to become "Investors in People". Agencies have been at the forefront in making their commitment and in introducing vocational qualifications programmes for their staff.

"Investors in People" in particular captures the current approach to training and development very well. It is a new National Standard in Britain to help businesses and services to get the best out of its people. It is based on the practical experience of businesses that have improved their performance through investing in people. An "Investor in People":

Makes public commitment from the top to develop all employees to achieve business objectives

- The employer should have a written but flexible plan which sets out business goals and targets, considers how employees will contribute to achieving the plan and specifies how development needs in particular will be assessed and met.

- Management should develop and communicate to all employees a vision of where the organisation is going and the contribution that employees will make to its success, involving employee representatives as appropriate.

Regularly reviews training and development needs of all employees

- The resources for training and developing employees should be clearly identified in the Business Plan.

- Managers should be responsible for regularly agreeing training and development needs with each employee in the context of business objectives, setting targets and standards linked, where appropriate, to the achievement of recognised qualifications.

Trains and develops individuals on recruitment and throughout their employment

- Action should focus on the training needs of all new recruits and continually developing and improving the skills of existing employees.

- All employees should be encouraged to contribute to identifying and meeting their own job-related development needs.

Evaluates the investment in training and development to assess achievement and improve future effectiveness

- The investment, the competence and commitment of employees, and the use made of skills learned should be reviewed at all levels against business goals and targets.
- The effectiveness of training and development should be reviewed at the top level and lead to renewed commitment and target-setting.

Most organisations have a lot of work to do to reach the standard.

The Vocational Qualification programme is built around the competence that staff in the two lowest grades in the Civil Service need to do their jobs based on national standards on administration and linked to a scheme which provides "National Vocational Qualifications".

There are direct links between this type of activity and setting criteria for recruitment and selection. There are also links with performance management and appraisal. Training is increasingly seen as an investment, rather than a cost, but is subject to all the usual business controls that govern investment decisions (i.e. what the return is likely to be).

For the public sector, as for all organisations, today's climate is bringing new challenges and an increasingly competitive environment, for example:

- higher quality expectations from customers;
- the need to respond to more rapid technological change;
- pressure to compete effectively with other organisations and to be seen to give good value for money in the market place;
- difficulties in recruiting young people or those older workers with the right skills.

1.3 Improving human resource management, including performance management and performance appraisal

This entry addresses three closely related aspects of human resource management. There are, also references to another closely-related subject – performance incentives – which is covered by a separate entry.

Personal Review (formerly staff appraisal) has taken on a broader management role in recent years. Hitherto, the appraisal system was primarily driven by personnel functions, and focused on efficiency checks, training needs and promotability assessments. Since the increased emphasis on rewarding for achievement (i.e. performance-related pay), the system has looked more to objective-setting, measurable outcomes, and the continuous dialogue between managers and staff. The development of core competence profiles and frameworks by which to assess outcomes, development needs and potential has also made an impact on how the appraisal system works.

The context for change

The centre of the U.K. Civil Service has been seeking to delegate ownership and autonomy as far as possible on this and many other areas of personnel/human resource management. The belief is that individual departments and Agencies have their own specific business needs, to which their management systems should be tailored. At the heart of performance management (which encompasses appraisal) is the integration of business goals with the most effective use of people.

Personnel functions are evolving such that they can enable managers to take on this wider role, and integrate the competencies of their staff with their organisational productivity.

For all but the top three grades in the Civil Service to which different arrangements apply, the centre sets out some rules which must be complied with and the principles which individual Departments and Agencies are expected to take into account when establishing their own appraisal and promotion arrangements. For appraisal there are two rules that must be complied with. These are:

i) The arrangements must include a means of rating overall performance which is unsatisfactory or unacceptable; and

ii) must underpin the organisation's arrangements for performance-related pay.

The principles to be taken into account are:

i) A system for regular appraisal is a key element in the delivery of results and improving the performance of people;

ii) The system should be appropriate to particular management and operational needs and should be reviewed regularly to ensure they are cost-effective;

iii) Staff should know in advance what is expected of them, how their performance will be assessed, and should get effective feedback: if assessment of fitness for promotion is made they should be informed;

iv) Those responsible for appraising people should be competent to do so and have received training;

v) Training and development needs should be identified where not established separately;

vi) There should be arrangements for recording and handling any disputes and management and staff should be aware of them.

Promotions must follow from a considered decision as to the fitness of individuals, on merit, to undertake the higher duties concerned. The principles that should be taken into account are:

i) The promotion arrangements should be appropriate to particular management and operational needs, and decisions on promotion should, unless unavoidable, take account of the judgement of more than one person;

ii) Promotion arrangements should be made known to staff, including the grounds for appeal and their right to do so;

iii) Common standards should be applied to all those who are being considered together in the same promotion exercise.

A range of other trends dovetail with the changes in the role of appraisal:

- competence-based human resource development (HRD), including the use of National Vocational Qualifications (NVQs);

- performance-related pay: the objective assessment of achievements on which to base rewards;

- delegation of human resource development (HRD) responsibilities to line managers;

- emphasis of Total Quality Management (TQM)/customer-focused management approaches. This is particularly important in Agencies with clear performance targets to meet. The Citizen's Charter and Next Steps initiatives each underline the importance of managing performance, which means managing all resources, including people, in clear and measurable ways.

A precursor of culture change in the U.K. was the Financial Management Initiative, which showed that managers were capable of taking authority for their budgeting decisions, and could control these effectively within clear parameters. This principle is now being extended to the HRD area.

Implementing change

If a complex, centralised public service bureaucracy is intending to delegate authority and empower individual organisations to deliver results to more specific standards, a clear policy steer from the top is needed. The building blocks of such change are:

- communication;
- systematic review;
- development of management capability (particularly in change and people-management areas).

Costs will depend on how far managers understand the costs of present levels of utilisation of people and whether hard performance targets are seriously negotiated and managed at senior level.

The "key stakeholders" include top managers and personnel functions. Each has to promote delegation, whilst at the same time empowering line managers in becoming the key stakeholder. To take people along, participative change management is required, i.e wide consultation, pilot work, flexible formats and a regular feedback on the progress of change.

Identification of risks/obstacles, as with any change programme, will involve an assessment of current climate, culture, attitudes, "champions", and levers on which to hinge the change. In any department or Agency, these will vary – at a central level, the change can be steered by a high-profile initiative manager, but this is not essential. In this area, management by results is itself a good route to demonstrating the benefit of change – it will only work where all other systems play to those rules.

Another key factor is the timing vis a vis other initiatives, e.g. market-testing or its equivalents. When major change is under way, performance management can be a helpful tool to reinforce it.

Appraisal system review, reform or creation can take a matter of months; much will depend on how far current systems fail to meet their stated purposes, and on the level of credibility that HRD Management has within the organisation(s). To effect real culture and behavioural changes, in whatever context, is recognised as being a much longer-term goal, and requires sustained vision and leadership.

In reviewing appraisal, typical steps involve:

- clarifying the purposes of the system;

- identifying the management processes which are in support of it or which it supports in turn (i.e management information systems, training and development programmes, planning cycles, grading structures and reward strategies etc);

- then a review of any existing forms, guidance and training. The extent to which the system drives or relates to other parts of the business will affect the length and depth of reform and resourcing in these area;

- wide consultation and involvement in design, implementation, evaluation and improvements is ideal: this may appear to be the slower and more costly route, but the end products are more cost-beneficial than an imposed system which fails to get better results from people.

1.4 Performance incentives in the public sector, including delegated pay bargaining

The U.K. Civil Service has been moving towards performance-related pay (PRP) as a performance incentive for several years. This was because it was thought important to recognise individuals' performance and encourage them to greater efforts by clarifying the direct link with pay increases. Pay increases irrespective of performance were wasteful and unproductive. Staff performing less than effectively had no incentive to change and indeed their lack of performance might not be exposed and dealt with at all.

All the new pay agreements have performance pay as their basis, to provide an annual link between pay and performance so that, each year, individuals' rewards reflect their performance. The schemes are dynamic and some involve more local discretion than others.

Under the new offers, all new money is to be put into the PRP budget, with departments having freedom over how to distribute the new element, and to negotiate this with the unions as necessary. Range maxima are to be increased significantly, so that the best performers will, over time, have significantly more scope to increase their earnings.

In the past, annual pay increases had largely been made irrespective of performance. The new agreements also include provision for flexibility to adjust pay bands for non-performance purposes, e.g. where there are recruitment/retention difficulties. There is also provision for delegating pay bargaining to individual departments and Agencies.

The context for change

The context of performance-related pay is provided by wider management developments currently under way in many parts of the public sector, such as the "Next Steps" initiative, the Citizen's Charter, contracting out and market-testing of services.

Pay delegation is also relevant and is described below.

Implementing change

U.K. experience shows that the really basic requirements or preconditions for successful action in this field include the following:

- determination to challenge the perceived right to automatic annual pay increases, irrespective of performance;
- careful, and probably lengthy, negotiations with the unions involved;
- careful explanation of the new system to the staff involved;
- a reliable and bias-free system of staff reporting, to assess performance accurately and fairly.

The costs of introducing a PRP system depend very much on what sort of system is wanted. A PRP system radically different from the pay system it replaced could in theory involve large new costs, both to set it up and then to run it. On the other hand, PRP could be introduced cost-neutrally: a scheme which linked rewards to achievements well would tend to offset its costs by its effects and so be justified in value for money terms.

The skills necessary to introduce a system include the following:

- negotiation with unions and staff;
- ability to set out clearly the staff reporting requirements and to train managers in their use;
- understanding the structure and dynamics of the organisation;
- ability to evaluate initial and long-term cost implications of proposals.

The key stakeholders, whose commitment is necessary for success, include:

- senior management;
- personnel managers with responsibility for performance-appraisal systems;
- personnel managers with responsibility for pay policy and systems;
- line managers.

Potential obstacles and risks include:

- failure to apply fair and consistent performance marking;

- inadequately trained managers do not apply a uniform standard across all the staff involved;

- annual pay increases may still be considered the norm and so there will be pressure to assess performance reasonably generously in order to achieve it;

- staff may feel that they are locked into a performance-related pay system and are not therefore free to move to new posts for fear of a drop in performance marking and so also of pay;

- staff may lose confidence in a pay system if it is not entirely transparent.

Progress in the U.K. has been achieved in stages, both in terms of the extent to which pay is related to performance, and the groups of staff to which it applies.

Accordingly, current systems have evolved since the mid-1980s. The latest substantial changes to systems where pay increases are fully related to performance were announced in principle by Ministers in mid-1991, embodied in new pay agreements during 1992, and implemented in 1992 or 1993, depending on the particular group of staff.

A particular initiative in introducing performance incentives: delegated pay bargaining

The U.K. Government is committed to delegate to departments and Agencies responsibility for the pay and grading of their own staff. This was announced by the Chancellor of the Exchequer in July 1991, and reflects Citizen's Charter initiatives. Pay delegation should:

- make pay more responsive to the market, and enable departments and Agencies to have greater control over their paybills whilst avoiding pay increases for the Civil Service or the public sector generally which are incompatible with the Government's policies for the economy and public spending;

- ensure that value for money is obtained from the Civil Service paybill, by promoting the delivery of high quality but affordable public services, and by rewarding good and penalising bad performance, within the framework of the Government's responsibilities as an employer and for the control of public expenditure; and

- increase transparency about pay costs.

The Civil Service (Management Functions) Act 1992 enables the Treasury to transfer its responsibility for setting terms and conditions to another Crown servant. Accordingly delegations of authority to negotiate pay and pay-related conditions of service ("pay delegations") will be made to the Minister (or in some cases the office-holder) in charge of a department or Agency: the larger Agencies, and some smaller ones, will assume responsibility for their own pay bargaining by April 1994. More pay delegations will follow in future years.

The general conditions attached to pay delegations are outlined in documentation agreed between the department or Agency and the Treasury at the time of the pay delegation (each individual Agency's "delegation instrument"). The conditions include adherence to a framework of controls ("the strategic control framework") within which delegated responsibility is to be managed. Details of each individual Agency's or department's particular control arrangements will be set out in a business case sent to the Treasury before delegation occurs. The operation of the control framework will require a continuing dialogue between the Agency or department in receipt of the delegation and the Treasury; it is the successful continuation of this which should achieve the Government's aims for pay delegation.

The strategic control framework is intended to ensure that delegated decisions do not increase upward pressure on public expenditure. Its main elements are:

- *the paybill control*: at the end of running costs negotiations, the planned paybill component of running costs is now identified more formally than in the past: it is used for monitoring purposes and to build up a track record; and

- *the negotiating remit*: this consists of the agreed limits and factors which define a department's or agency's authority to negotiate pay and pay-related conditions of service: it is agreed between the department or Agency and the Treasury shortly before pay negotiations begin.

The recently published White Paper "The Civil Service: Continuity and Change" reaffirmed the policy of increased delegation and disaggregation and of reduced central control. This is based on the view that comprehensive systems are no longer best suited to a Civil Service which carries out a hugh number of different tasks and delivers a wide range of services. Delegated pay and grading systems can be more flexible and more closely tailored to the needs of the organisation. In particular there should be a clear link between the individual's pay and their contribution to the achievement of the organisation's objectives. It is proposed that by April 1996 responsibility for the pay and grading of staff below senior levels should be delegated to all departments and the existing national pay arrangements replaced. the government would also like each Agency, within a department, to be responsible for its own pay and grading. For senior staff (grade 5 and above) it is proposed that pay should be individually determined on the basis of a number of overlapping pay ranges broadly linked to levels of responsibility. Individual Permanent Secretaries would control the pay progression of their staff taking account of performance, level of responsibility and marketability of their skills and experience. The operation of the system would be monitored centrally and adjusted as necessary to ensure coherence between departments. Control of cost would be exercised through the overall departmental paybill.

1.5 Mission orientation

Mission orientation seeks to provide clear and understandable goals which are accepted by operational staff and are fully owned by senior managers. Mission-oriented culture (engendering energy and creativity), results in an achieving and pro-active, rather than controlling and re-active, public service.

The context for change

The purpose in establishing mission orientation is to:

- clarify the purpose of the business in the minds of management, so that resources are accurately channelled towards achieving the precise goals;
- clarify for staff the purpose of their jobs in meeting organisational goals;
- make clear the policy of the government of the day to ensure that it is interpreted accurately by staff;
- to engender pride in the department and a sense of belonging to an organisation with a purpose;
- within individual businesses, provide a target to aim for and against which to assess actions and results.

Each individual in the organisation needs to know and understand clear goals. Managers must aim to ensure that all are working in the same direction to achieve the organisation's goals.

Implementing change

The U.K. Civil Service has over recent years made considerable efforts in the area of customer service and in trying to bring to staff the mission orientation of clear goals and purposes. A number of departments and Agencies have produced Mission Statements and Core Values, based on organisational needs. At an individual level, individual businesses within the department have prepared their own mission statements, to provide a focus for staff efforts at local level.

This topic is inevitably linked with quality management and indeed mission orientation is a critical part of achieving a successful quality programme. Quality programmes require managers to behave differently in managing the process and it follows also that staff need to be carefully led into and trained in mission concepts.

The U.K. experience suggests that the basic requirements or pre-conditions for successful action in this field include the following:

- understanding customer needs;
- top management commitment to goals expressed in the mission statement, based on meeting the requirements of the customers;
- clear understanding by management and staff of mission concepts;
- full explanations and training available to staff to supplement the mission statements.

Costs will depend on the size and extent of the mission orientation project and the methods used to involve staff. They will include the cost of compiling and drafting the mission statement and circulating material to staff. Videos are sometimes used and can be quite expensive.

The skills required for achieving a mission orientation would include the following:

- top management modelling the behaviour required by the staff - action, not just words;
- far-sighted management, able to convey aims and objectives in a way which will be meaningful to staff at all levels;
- close co-operation with trade unions and staff;
- clear, plain language material which conveys the mission concepts clearly and powerfully to staff;
- an ability to convey corporate pride and image as part of achieving the sense of mission among staff.

Key stakeholders include, primarily, senior managers in the organisation concerned. However, publicity staff also need to be active in preparing display material and easily understood text.
Potential obstacles include the following:

- staff believing that the mission concept is "just another initiative";

- management and staff failing to take the mission concept seriously;
- allowing the statement of objectives or mission statement to become outdated or irrelevant, by failing to review and redraft it regularly;
- trade union opposition;
- resources to carry it through.

Drafting a mission statement for a small business or department within government is rarely achieved in less than one to two months, because of the need to consult quite extensively among management and staff and to check and reconsider the draft several times to ensure that it is right and to get it agreed by Ministers. Printing and disseminating material will of course also take a few weeks. Revising the objectives each year (or for changes of government) will probably also take a month or so, while drafts are agreed.

A summary of the typical steps or stages in introducing mission orientation is:

- top management participation in a facilitated workshop to contemplate the aims and purposes of the department;
- vision established where the department is now and where it wants to be in three or five years' time;
- aims set out in understandable and meaningful words;
- material tested with Ministers and staff;
- material refined and publicised (handout/staff newspaper/poster in building foyers/video);
- vision and objectives explained very fully to staff and participation invited.

1.6 Recruitment and retention

Recruitment to the Civil Service must be conducted in accordance with Treasury requirements and the Minister for the Civil Service's rules on selection on merit on the basis of fair and open competition (unless one of the permitted exceptions applies). The Civil Service Commissioners advise the Minister on the content of the rules and monitor their application by departments and Agencies.

Since 1991 departments and Agencies have had responsibility for recruiting over ninety five per cent of their staff within the framework laid down by the Civil Service Order in Council 1991. On other appointments in senior and fast-stream grades which are specified in Schedule I of the Order and any ungraded posts regarded as "special appointments", departments must consult the independent Civil Service Commissioners. The Commissioners must in general give their written approval before such an appointment can be made from outside the Service. Where a post at Grade 3 level or above is to be filled by open competition this must be reported in advance to the Cabinet Office.

Treasury approval is required for the creation of any new grade or grading structure. In addition, the Civil Service Commissioners must be notified of any newly approved departmental grades above the level of Senior Executive Officer, of any new fast stream feeder grades and of any changes in the titles of departmental grades at these levels.

There are six Civil Service Commissioners. At present two are full-time civil servants. Since 1978 other Commissioners have been drawn from outside the Civil Service in order to provide experience of good personnel management practice in the private sector; they serve part-time, normally for periods of three or four years each. The Commissioners are appointed under the Royal Prerogative, not under Statute, as part of the Executive. They derive their powers from the Civil Service, and Diplomatic Service, Orders in Council, 1991. The Orders promulgate the Government's general policy in respect of entry to the two Services – no appointments may be made unless selection has been carried out "on merit on the basis of fair and open competition". All appointments are made by Ministers or on their behalf. In respect of certain defined grades the Orders provide that the Commissioners' approval is a precondition of appointment; the Commissioners base their approval on the knowledge that in each case selection has been conducted in accordance with the policy. The Commissioners act independently of Ministers when giving or withholding approval in individual cases, and are personally answerable for the decisions they reach. The Commissioners report annually on their work to the Queen, not to Parliament, and their report is published.

The Orders set out the scope of the Commissioners' responsibilities broadly as follows:

- approval of candidates before senior appointments (Grade 7 level and above) and appointments to the fast-stream feeder entries can be made;
- rules in respect of selection to those appointments;
- advice to the Minister for the Civil Service and the Foreign Secretary on the formal Rules, made by the two Ministers, to govern the selection procedures to be followed by departments and Agencies when making appointments at grade levels below those controlled by the Commissioners;
- monitoring the way departments and Agencies apply the Minister's Rules.

The Commissioners' powers do not extend beyond the Home Civil Service and Diplomatic Service to the Northern Ireland Civil Service or to any other part of the public service, and involve no Service-wide personnel management functions other than selection for first appointment.

The First Commissioner, as a senior official in the Cabinet Office (Office of Public Service and Science) also has administrative responsibility for central liaison with the careers services of schools and universities, and for advising the Minister for the Civil Service on nationality rules and character standards for entry to the Civil Service.

The context for change

The policy and practice of selection on merit by fair and open competition ensure that Civil Service recruitment provides equal opportunity for employment, regardless of race, gender or marital status. They also take account of government policy on the employment of people registered as disabled.

The policy of selection on merit on the basis of fair and open competition has endured since the reforms of the mid-nineteenth century. It remains valid as a means of providing an effective, non-political, Civil Service. But over the last decade or so there have been substantial changes in the way in which recruitment is managed. Responsibility for carrying out the vast majority of recruitment has been transferred to departments and their new Agencies, subject to observance of the Minister's rules on selection and to any other centrally laid down requirements. The thrust of the recruitment changes in 1991 was to give managers more freedom to select and recruit the staff they needed for the new tasks and ways of working the Civil Service. At the same time, they were designed to ensure that the

Commissioners had the powers they needed to safeguard the principle of selection on merit on the basis of fair and open competition.

The delegation of recruitment criteria from the centre allows departments to prescribe what is most appropriate for their needs. Some departments, for example, are moving away from qualification-based criteria to a system based on identifying what 'competencies' are needed for the job in question and recruiting people who most closely fit that range of skills and experience.

To comply with the requirements for fair and open competition departments must:

- give prospective applicants a reasonable opportunity to become aware of the vacancies and a reasonable time within which to apply;
- consider all eligible applicants equally on merit at all stages of the selection process, under procedures providing safeguards against individual bias;
- ensure that all selection criteria and techniques are reliable, valid and relevant to the jobs or grades concerned.

Before departments make an unconditional offer of appointment, they must check each candidate's eligibility (including, as appropriate: age, education, professional attainment, nationality, health and character).

Implementing change

Prior to 1964, the Civil Service Commission was responsible for all Civil Service recruitment. It first delegated to departments recruitment for clerical posts in shortage areas to speed up the process. By 1982 the delegation had been extended to most recruits below Executive Officer level (roughly eighty-five per cent of the total) and the Commission confined its activity largely to checking certain aspects of eligibility before issuing the certification of qualification to appoint. The prerequisite for appointment of a Commissioners' certificate of qualification was withdrawn for those grades in 1982 and responsibility for selection was divided between the commissioners and Ministers. With effect from 1 January 1983, departments assumed, on behalf of their Ministers, responsibility for selection at junior levels, i.e. most recruitment, subject to instructions by the Minister for the Civil Service about appointment on merit by means of open competition.

This process was carried a step further in 1991 when departments were given responsibility for recruitment at middle level as well. At the same time, it was decided that the recruitment activity of the former Civil Service Commission was a suitable candidate for Agency status. In April 1991 the Commission was replaced by two separate organisations:

- a small Office of the Civil Service Commission to support the Commissioners;

- the Recruitment and Assessment Services Agency to undertake, on full repayment and in competition with other recruiters, most of the executive recruitment and assessment function previously handled by the former Civil Service Commission, along with a broad range of related services, including professional consultancy and research services on selection methods.

These changes were announced to Parliament nearly two years before they were implemented.

Responsibility for prescribing recruitment criteria for all grades except those listed in Schedule 1 of the Order was delegated to Ministers and statutory office holders in charge of departments on 4 May 1993. Departments and Agencies must ensure that their recruitment systems consistently deliver recruits who:

- are appropriate to the organisation's needs; and

- are able to do the work required in the grade to which they are appointed.

The delegation of, for example, recruitment criteria gives departments a welcome new tool for setting up arrangements that are appropriate to their particular situation. But delegation does not end the Treasury's involvement. Where departments have set up competence-based (rather than qualification-based) systems, the Treasury have acted in an advisory capacity to help departments, not least by facilitating the spread of best practice. For action to be successful it is not always enough merely to delegate, it is also important to ensure that recipients have proper systems (and the skills to go with them) in place, or that they are available.

Departments must maintain records for at least three years of the recruitment criteria in use at each grade level and of the performance of successful candidates. The Treasury is therefore able to fulfil its continuing responsibility to ensure that quality is maintained by monitoring recruitment schemes.

The respective responsibilities of the Civil Service Commissioners and the Recruitment and Assessment Services Agency have been reviewed and it is proposed that:

- departments and Agencies should be responsible for undertaking recruitment at all levels and accountable for recruiting in accordance with the principles of openness, fairness and merit;

- the Civil Service Commissioners should be responsible for regulating recruitment at all levels and for acting as custodians of the principles of openness, fairness and merit;

- The Office of Public Services and Science should be responsible for exercising such corporate management functions as need to be retained centrally.

The Government has welcomed the proposals.

As far as retention of staff is concerned, the U.K. Government has relied on those areas where it is perceived a "good" employer – provision of training equal opportunities, pension rights, special allowances for IT staff etc. In locations where there is a lot of competition among employers, the Government has given Local Pay Additions, which are specifically targeted at recruitment and retention.

1.7 Anti-corruption measures

Corruption is a crime that anyone can commit and the offences are not confined to the actions of civil servants. It is essentially a criminal matter, rather than one of conduct and discipline. Departments draw the attention of their staff to the Prevention of Corruption Acts 1907 and 1916. However, the 1916 Act provided that, where an alleged offence related to government contracts and a gift or other consideration was proved to have been received by an employee of the Crown or any public body from a contractor (or would-be contractor), the onus lay on the defence to prove that the gift or consideration was not given or received corruptly. Thus the law bears more heavily here on civil servants and those with whom they deal because, in the case of a gift given or received within the private sector, the burden of proof, as in the general criminal law, is on the prosecution.

There are stringent rules set out in Chapter 4 of the Civil Service Management Code to ensure that civil servants act with propriety and avoid any suspicion of corruption or bias. The rules require not simply that civil servants must not accept open bribes, but also that many less blatant and often apparently innocent gestures, such as the acceptance of hospitality and general favours, are also avoided. Among the measures in place to address the question of bias and corruption in its broadest sense are the following:

- Civil servants must not make use of their official position to further their private interests or those of others. They are also required to avoid conflicts of interest which may arise from financial interests, freemasonry etc.;

- Civil servants must not receive gifts, hospitality or benefits of any kind which might be seen to compromise their personal judgement or integrity;

- There are rules covering the employment by third parties of former civil servants, to avoid the risk that a particular firm might gain advantage over its competitors by employing someone with specialist knowledge and to avoid the suspicion that a civil servant's decisions might be influenced by the promise or expectation of future employment.

The purpose of the law and regulations is to maintain the historical reputation enjoyed by the U.K. Civil Service for its impartiality and its ability to serve governments of different persuasions with equal commitment and efficiency. The intention is to avoid not merely actual corruption but any actions which could be construed as potentially corrupting.

Any change would be a legislative, rather than administrative process. It would be ineffective to rely only on disciplinary sanctions for public servants in the absence of any wider criminal sanction for those outside who might seek to corrupt them. So action here would involve preparing legislation and fitting it into Parliamentary timescales. It would be difficult to commend the U.K.'s current Prevention of Corruption Acts as such. They have obscurities and the 1916 Act is generally acknowledged as hasty wartime legislation.

Supporting material

(i) Prevention of Corruption Acts 1906, Ch 34, ISBN 0-11-802098-6, £0.30, 1979 (Statutes in force edition)

(ii) Prevention of Corruption Act 1916, Ch 64, ISBN 0-11-802100-1, £0.20, 1979 (Statutes in force edition)

1.8 Developing a Public Service Code of Conduct

This entry covers only the procedures which apply to civil servants in a narrow definition. It does not cover, for example, members and staff of non-departmental public bodies, who are not civil servants. Broadly equivalent rules apply to such staff. Nor does the entry apply to Ministers, who are expected to follow separate guidance in Questions of Procedures for Ministers.

In the U.K., civil servants are civilian employees, with effectively the same status as other employees. Conduct and discipline rules are framed in the wider context of employment law and have to pay due regard to it, not least because civil servants have the same legal remedies as others in matters such as unfair dismissal. A different legal background in other countries might prompt other approaches.

Rules framed as conditions of service can carry no penalty greater than dismissal. It follows also that those who have already left are beyond reach. The U.K. Civil Service Pension Scheme has no provision for forfeiture of rights as a consequence of disciplinary action. Superannuation benefits can be withdrawn only if a civil servant or former civil servant is convicted of certain serious criminal offences, and automatic loss of pension rights occurs only in the case of a conviction for treason. Where misconduct becomes criminal, sanctions are a wider legal issue.

Different considerations apply if considering employees with any other status, for example, that of the armed services (with their own statutory provisions for disciplinary matters and their own systems of justice), or to a lesser extent that of the police. The central framework derives from the need for civil servants to be, and to be seen to be, honest and impartial in the exercise of their duties. They must not allow their judgement or integrity to be compromised in fact or by reasonable implication.

A central framework of rules to govern the conduct of civil servants is contained in Chapter 4 of the Civil Service Management Code, which came into effect on 1 February 1993. The Code covers:

- the duty not to misuse official information;
- political neutrality;
- conflicts of interest;
- the duties of civil servants in relation to Ministers;
- rules on acceptance of business appointments.

The new Code re-ordered and simplified previous material to clarify the key principles, but it did not make changes of substance. The central framework does not attempt to be a comprehensive code of conduct. It does not deal, for example, with such issues as isolated neglect of duty, failure to obey a reasonable instruction, or other forms of misconduct which may properly be dealt with under disciplinary arrangements. Departments and Agencies must define the standard of conduct they require of their staff, incorporating the framework, and adding any further rules necessary to reflect local needs and circumstances.

Adherence to the rules is a condition of service. Breaches are subject to disciplinary action with penalties up to and including dismissal. The sanctions to be applied as a result of disciplinary proceedings are not prescribed centrally and are a matter for the department or Agency concerned, in the light of the circumstances of each case.

In addition to conduct rules, civil servants are subject to relevant criminal laws, like other citizens. Those include:

- Prevention of Corruption Acts 1906 and 1916;
- Official Secrets Acts 1911 (section 1) and 1989;
- Company Securities (Insider Dealing) Act 1985;
- Financial Services Act 1986.

The context for change

The Civil Service is currently the subject of an enquiry by the Treasury and Civil Service Select Committee of the House of Commons. Evidence already taken by the Committee illustrates a debate on the adequacy of current rules of conduct as a result of developments in the Service, such as the creation of Executive Agencies, vesting powers in non-elected bodies, market-testing and privatisation. Concern has also been expressed about the effect on the Civil Service of a long period of government by a single party.

In the context of the Committee's enquiry, there has been much argument for and against the adoption of a formal code of ethics, and indeed some would have Civil Service responsibilities and conduct enshrined in an Act of Parliament. Ministers do not currently favour this approach. Arguments against include:

- difficulty in covering all aspects of Civil Service conduct in a single, all-embracing code;

- difficulties in enshrining even the fundamental values of the Service – impartiality, integrity, objectivity, selection and promotion on merit – because even basic principles need to be qualified, for example:
  - selection on merit does not strictly apply to casual staff or Ministers' special advisers;
  - political impartiality does not apply to the politically free group, and applies in varying degrees to other groups, both by grade and type of work.
- the present system is flexible, and has proved responsive to a variety of demands over the years. There have been 14 changes since 1980 and few years pass without one or more amendments. Where changes have been suggested, Government has been able to react positively;
- legislation is less flexible, and Civil Service bills to effect amendments could not be expected to have high priority in any Government's legislative programme.

Reasons for changes to rules of conduct and examples include:

- to reflect legislative changes, for example the new Official Secrets Act 1989 and the Copyright Act 1988;
- to reflect public or Parliamentary concerns, for example the Business Appointments Rules, introduced in the 1930s and frequently revised since;
- to amplify and clarify guidance, for example the Armstrong Memorandum, summarised in the Rules since 1985 and now incorporated in full in the Code;
- as part of wider revisions of Civil Service codes (in 1944, 1974 and 1993).

Supporting material

(i) 6th Report of the Treasury and Civil Service Committee, "The Role of the Civil Service: Interim Report" (House of Commons 1992-93 Paper 390 - I), ISBN 0-10-022433-4, £8.10

(ii) There is also a supporting volume of evidence published in August 1993 (House of Commons Paper 1992-93 390 - II), ISBN 0-10-022803-8, HMSO, £32.50

1.9 Contractual employment

This entry covers the varying terms under which U.K. civil servants are employed, few of which are in the true sense contractual. The great majority of UK civil servants are employed on a full-time, permanent basis, although they do not have a contract of employment as such. Terms and conditions are indicated in a formal letter of appointment, which relates to rules set out in the Civil Service Management Code. It is the Government's intention that their employees enjoy the same employment protection as any other employee.

The context for change

In 1987, the Mueller Report examined the evidence for the view that working patterns were becoming increasingly flexible in the private sector and assessed the implications for the future of working patterns in the Civil Service. Another factor, coming a year or so later, was a growing realisation about the impact of demographic changes on the labour market. The Mueller Report found that in the private sector:

- many people did not work a standard week;
- the range of alternative working patterns was increasing;
- there was a significant trend towards more imaginative use of part-time working;
- organisations needed to reduce their running costs and did so by matching staff costs with work as closely as possible.

It concluded that the solution was to tap the pool of high quality people who could not – or did not wish to – commit themselves to full five-day week working. The Report recommended introducing new working patterns, in particular for temporary work and home working and wider use of existing working patterns. As a result, departments would be free to tailor working patterns to almost any departmental/individual need with terms and conditions of service that were as attractive as necessary.

However, two years after the Mueller Report, there was little evidence that departments had moved much beyond the wider use of existing working patterns, in particular casuals and part-time work. They perceived that they were tied down by restrictive legislation and Civil Service rules. The Treasury therefore agreed to draw up guidance which introduced the categories of Recurring Temporary

Appointment, Short Notice Appointments, Standby Appointments and Home Working.

It has been increasingly recognised that effectively used, more varied patterns of working should offer benefits to management and staff. They are intended to help departments and Agencies to use and develop their most important resource – their staff – as effectively as possible and to respond more readily to likely changes, for example in the supply of labour, in the years ahead. These include demographic changes, economic and social pressures bringing, for example, more women with family responsibilities into the employment market and the realisation that inflexible full-time employment arrangements can under some circumstances be wasteful and expensive.

Implementing change

Increasingly, civil servants are being employed on other patterns of work and types of appointment, which include the following:

Conditional appointments
Appointments can be made on a conditional basis when, at the time of making the appointment, the full conditions for appointment on a permanent basis or fixed-term appointment have either not been met or verified. The appointment is offered conditionally, subject to the candidate satisfactorily meeting the conditions in due course.

Part-time working (including job sharing)
The amount of part-time working in the Civil Service has grown considerably over recent years. There are now more than 32,000 non-industrial and industrial staff working part-time hours. Part-time working involves working less than the conditioned hours (normally 41/42 per week) of the grade, while job sharing involves sharing (or splitting) the responsibilities of one full-time job between two or more people. This type of arrangement is becoming increasingly popular as people combine work and private responsibilities.

Fixed-term appointments
Fixed-term appointments (FTAs) are appointments which are made for a specified period of time. In British law, they must have defined start and expiry dates. Such arrangements are used in the Civil Service only where there is a genuine management need to make an appointment of limited duration, rather than a permanent appointment. For example, the task may be of limited duration or there is a short-term need to employ staff for a particular period.

Casual appointments
Casual appointments are temporary appointments to meet short-term needs. Departments may use casuals only where there is a genuine management need to employ people for a short period, rather than make a permanent appointment. For example, they may need to cover unexpected increases in workloads, maternity leave, prolonged sick leave or to help re-deploy staff in the case of the closure of an office. In general, the maximum length of a continuous casual appointment is 12 months, but it can of course be less.

Recurring temporary appointments
These are arrangements under which staff are contracted to work for short periods each year. The dates of employment for each year and the number of years for which the employment is offered are agreed in advance and set out in the letter of appointment. Such appointments can be useful when a department needs extra staff at certain periods of the year, for example to cover peak periods of work or to provide back-up when staff are absent on leave and work cannot be held over.

Employing people to work at short notice
This arrangement allows managers to employ people to work at short notice, usually for short periods at a time. It may be used when a department needs extra staff to cover unforeseen or temporary shortages of permanent staff, or to deal with tasks which occur on a irregular basis. This might include covering sick absences or annual leave, covering short-term peaks of work or offering work to former members of staff who have retired but would still like to work for short periods.

Standby appointments
This is a more formal arrangement than short notice employment. Under standby appointments, people contract to make themselves available for work for short periods each year and to accept work whenever they are called upon, subject to an agreed period of notice. The dates of employment for each year, the number of years for which employment is offered and the period of notice before each work assignment are all agreed in advance and set out in the letter of appointment.

The U.K. Government is open to innovative forms of employment and there is now increasing freedom for staff to work flexible hours and sometimes from home.

Organisational structure and culture determine the types of contract within the organisation. For example, a government Agency with short-term needs may choose to use fixed-term contracts extensively. It is also important for the public service to be sensitive to economic and social pressures among the workforce and to any competing (and possibly more attractive) arrangements being offered by the private sector. The keynote is a move towards flexibility, an understanding of organisational objectives and employees' reasonable expectations. It is obviously important to involve any Trades Union representatives at an early stage in any proposed reform.

In the U.K. Civil Service, the changes have taken place over the past six to eight years. Mueller reported in 1987, yet two years later the various obstacles referred to above meant that only limited progress had been made. It took a further two years to increase flexibilities and issue Treasury guidance. Even now, the uptake of the full extent of flexibilities is taking time to gather full momentum.

1.10 Workforce size control

Up to 1985, HM Treasury sought to control the administrative costs of government by imposing staffing ceilings on departments. The system was replaced by controls on the running costs of departments. Departments are expected to meet all their administration costs from within their running costs limits.

The main emphasis in the control of departments' resources is on cash provision for running costs, so staff figures are indicative control totals and not control limits. Most running costs expenditure is controlled gross, but since 1991-2, net running costs limits have operated in certain areas where expenditure and receipts vary in line with demand. Rather than impose arbitrary reductions from the centre, and adversely affect services, the desired outcome of reducing expenditure on running costs is better achieved through tight cash planning.

The context for change

The Government has a commitment to ensure public sector services from whichever sources, including the private sector, provide best value for money.

Imposing staffing ceilings was found to be a crude approach, which on occasions encouraged departments to contract out work at added cost. The objective of running costs control is to keep expenditure on administration under proper control, continue the downward pressure on these costs and encourage the search for greater efficiency. An overriding concern of workforce size control is of course also to deliver value for money to the taxpayer.

There is a link with developments in management within departments, including devolved budgeting and the establishment of Executive Agencies. Many services traditionally performed in-house within government departments have already been contracted out or are being market-tested. Contractorisation takes administrative expenditure out of running costs and takes staff out of the Civil Service staff count.

Implementing change

Plans for each department are agreed during the Public Expenditure Survey and are set out in departmental reports. Running costs expenditure is clearly identified in Supply Estimates.

Essential prerequisites include:

- suitably robust monitoring and management systems;
- desired reductions in staffing requirements should not be achieved at the cost of impairing services to the public.

As the process continues, the staffing requirements of central government will continue to fall. Those staff remaining will increasingly have their pay linked directly to performance. (Performance-related pay is dealt with in a separate entry in this series.)

In the U.K., Civil Service staff numbers fell by more than five per cent between 1985-86 and 1991-92. Numbers continue to fall and now stand at 533,350. Many departments envisage staffing reductions of over twenty per cent in the next two to three years. The share of public spending taken up by running costs is expected to fall from 8.9 per cent in 1992-93 to 8.0 per cent by 1995-96. The recently published White Paper, "The Civil Service: Continuity and Change" says that the Government expects the number of civil servants to fall to significantly below 500,000 on present trends.

Supporting material

i) Departmental Reports (an example – DTI – Cm 2204, available from HMSO), ISBN 0-10-122042-1, £12.85

ii) Public Expenditure Analysis to 1995-96: statistical supplement to the 1992 Autumn statement – Cm 2219, HMSO, ISBN 0-10-122192-4, £19.50

iii) White Paper "Competing for Quality", HMSO – Cm 1730, ISBN 0-10-117302-4, £6.85, 1991

iv) Citizen's Charter, HMSO – Cm 1599, ISBN 0-10-115992-7, £8.50

v) White Paper "The Civil Service: Continuity and Change" – Cm 2627, HMSO, ISBN 0-10-126272-8, £7.10

1.11 Redundancy management

British civil servants have no entitlement to statutory redundancy pay, and other aspects of statutory redundance provisions do not apply to the Crown. Nevertheless, the usual practice for departments is to act consistently with the relevant statutory provisions.

Government departments recognise the importance that staff attach to secure employment, and do their best, including future planning of staff requirements, to avoid the need for redundancy. Where redundancies are inevitable, departments continue to make every reasonable effort to minimise the number of employees made redundant compulsorily. These include transfers of surplus staff to other work areas; restrictions on recruitment and/or promotion; review of the use of casual and/or contract employees; reduction or elimination of overtime; retraining of staff for redeployment to other work where vacancies exist; allowing surplus staff to block temporarily vacant posts in lower grades; downgrading or regrading staff; inviting staff to volunteer for redundancy on compulsory carly retirement/severance terms; review of age retirement practice.

The context for change

Under the Employment Protection (Consolidation) Act, 1978, a dismissal is only for redundancy if the reason or principal reason is that:

- the employer has ceased, or intends to cease, to carry on the business for the purposes of which the employer was employed; or
- the employer has ceased, or intends to cease, to carry on the business in the place where the employee was so employed; or
- the requirements of the business for employees to carry out work of a particular kind have ceased or diminished or are expected to cease or diminish; or
- the requirements of the business for employees to carry out work of a particular kind, in the place where they were so employed, have ceased or diminished or are expected to cease or diminish.

Implementing change

The position concerning the responsibility for redundancy has changed considerably in recent years, with a centralised system, under HM Treasury, being replaced by a decentralised system under which individual departments have considerable freedom to act within a specific framework document 'Redundancy: Principles and Procedures', issued by the Treasury in September 1991.

Departments are responsible for negotiating and operating redundancy arrangements, and implement any redundancies accordingly. Departments are not required to consult HM Treasury before negotiating an agreement or implementing redundancies. Both HM Treasury and the departments believe that departments' freedom to take key decisions results in redundancy being operated in a more efficient way than under a centralised system.

Departmental staff who volunteer for redundancy, or who are compelled to leave on grounds of redundancy, are eligible to receive the appropriate benefits under the Principal Civil Service Pension Scheme (PCSPS). Departments do not have the scope to vary the terms of the PCSPS, but there are a number of discretionary items which they are free to use in managing staff reductions, if they believe their use would add value for money. HM Treasury does not monitor the ways in which departments use these discretions.

Departments bear the costs of early retirement or redundancy, and so are directly accountable for the expenditure.

Where there is a clear need for redundancies, departments should handle the redundancies taking account of statutory requirements and good industrial relations practice.

The Advisory, Conciliation and Arbitration Service (ACAS), provides guidance in the area of industrial relations. It is an independent statutory body, established under the Employment Protection Act 1975, with the general duty of promoting the improvement of industrial relations and has issued advice on redundancy handling.

ACAS advises all employers to adopt a formal policy on redundancy which sets out the approach for management to adopt when faced with making redundancies. In some cases it may be appropriate to negotiate an agreement on the procedure to be followed.

Where it is decided to establish a redundancy procedure, departments will need to consult on its contents. This procedure may include:

- a statement of intent to avoid compulsory redundancies wherever possible;

details of consultation arrangements;

- measures to avoid or minimise compulsory redundancies;
- a general statement of the selection criteria that may be adopted when compulsory redundancy is unavoidable;
- a reference to the financial benefits available to redundant staff;
- details of any appeal or hardship procedures.

The key players involved in actions to implement a redundancy policy are likely to be departmental (government) ministers, senior management, trade union representatives, and staff (both those who may be affected by redundancy and those responsible for such 'personnel' matters as pay and conditions of service).

It is important to secure the necessary internal authority for a redundancy policy, and to devise a phased action plan that takes the policy forward on a structured basis and allows notification to the relevant parties of what will or may happen, with the necessary consultation, at a sufficiently early stage when it is apparent that compulsory redundancies will be necessary, departments need to decide the unit of redundancy and the criteria for selecting staff. The criteria for determining the unit of redundancy may include:

- grade;
- specialism/discipline;
- geographic location;
- functional area of work;
- other relevant factors.

The criteria for selecting staff may include:

- ***skills or qualifications***: to ensure retention of a balanced staffing profile appropriate to future needs. Selection must be objective, and other aptitudes may need to be taken into account;
- ***individual ability***: ability or specialist knowledge acquired from special training at the department's expense, or an individual's value to the department's objectives;
- ***standard of work performance***: selection must be supported by objective evidence, e.g. by appraisal assessments;

- ***attendance or disciplinary records:*** absence records must be accurate, and reasons investigated;

- ***seniority or length of service:*** selection, by definition, is objective, and is usually used when there is no other way of distinguishing between employees.

The criteria should be objective, consistently applied and not based solely on the opinion of an individual line manager. When applied, they should cover all employees concerned in the unit of redundancy, including anyone who may be absent. Departments should carefully examine the implications of any selection procedure to ensure that unlawful discrimination does not result either directly or indirectly.

Departments should consider whether to establish an appeal procedure for staff who claim that their selection for redundancy is unfair, or whether such claims should be raised under the existing departmental grievance procedure.

Departments may arrange, for redundant staff, resettlement/counselling facilities to assist in their finding alternative employment etc.

The Civil Service Management Code sets down the minimum periods of notice. Where it is not possible to give the minimum period of notice, staff may be given compensation in lieu of notice.

1.12 Human resource information systems

A human resource information system may also be called a 'staff records system', or a 'personnel records system'. According to the nature of the government service and local practice, human resource information may be held on a central basis (i.e. it covers staff in all departments) or on a decentralised basis (i.e. individual departments have their own records and are responsible for their maintenance and modification). In the United Kingdom, individual government departments maintain their own records.

The context for change

The Government, or department, needs a human resource information system in order to carry out its functions as employer efficiently, and, by implication, to operate aspects of its administration (e.g. its payroll) efficiently.

The employer is likely to require staff information for both strategic purposes, e.g. if a regional sub-office is to be created and an assessment of possible staff to work there is being made, and purposes that simply concern an individual (e.g. whether he or she has the correct qualifications for a particular posting, or how to contact him/her out of office hours). Ideally, therefore, the system which is in place should be able to reveal the required information, or be able to be 'interrogated', with the minimum of effort.

Increasing pressures for flexibility are encouraging the departments to introduce computerised human resource information systems to be used with other management information systems (either within a particular department or with another department) and to assess the extent to which information on the differing areas needs to be married together and produced on a common basis.

Implementing change

U.K. experience suggests that for a paper or computer-based system, the information needed by the employer includes:

- number of staff
  - by different grades;
  - by terms of their employment, e.g. full-time or part-time;

- location of staff
  - by blocks of staff, e.g. Division/Branch/Regional Office;
  - by individual;
- details of individual members of staff, e.g.
  - names (in full);
  - dates of birth;
  - home addresses;
  - emergency contacts;
  - skills;
  - work preferences;
  - qualifications;
  - language(s) knowledge;
  - career histories;
  - pay;
  - staff appraisal reports;
  - sick leave records;
  - promotion board results;
  - training courses attendance;
  - disabilities.

Project management techniques are used when major management information systems are being introduced. The following are key ingredients in the implementation of any such system:

- establish an action committee (project board), its members being individuals who have a direct interest in – or can exert a positive influence upon – the successful implementation of the project (e.g. senior managers, technical experts and system users);
- ensure that the necessary finance for the project is in place or will be available when needed;
- define project objectives (including user requirements);

- develop an action plan (setting down what is to be achieved at what time, and by whom);

- consider the need for a tender to be issued (if project implementation is to be carried out by an outside or private firm or body, and bids are to be assessed to determine which gives the greatest value for money etc.);

- consider advertising for 'expressions of interest' (i.e. from outside bodies/firms), if the project is to go forward on the basis of competitive tender;

- devise tender specifications (if appropriate) and issue the tender or advertise tender-documents availability;

- evaluate the bids which have resulted from the issue of any tender;

- establish a contract with the chosen supplier (successful bidder);

- ensure that implementation-review procedures are in place to be certain that any problems are identified and modifications made at a sufficiently early stage;

- start project implementation.

A particular initiative in introducing a human resource information sytem: The Department of Trade and Industry

By the early 1980s the development and commercial availability of computer systems were well established and their advantages in facilitating work practices were very apparent. Until this time the Department of Trade and Industry (DTI) kept only paper-based personnel management records of its staff. In 1983 a study team recommended the development of computerised systems in a number of key areas in the DTI to provide operational and management information to assist with the management of resources. They were to incorporate a number of basic principles:

- each user was to be responsible for the validity and relevance of the information in the systems;

- prime users were to have prompt and easy access to the system;

- relevant information was to be made widely available, subject to essential security and privacy requirements;

- data entry was to involve the minimum of duplication;

- a modular approach was to be adopted in which core blocks were to be developed and then extended by the addition of related segments.

Following approval by a top-level DTI committee, and the creation of a Project Board, the Personnel Management Information System (PERMIS) project began in 1983. Its objectives were:

- to provide a central staff records system for personnel management staff;

- to interface with other DTI computer systems relating to finance, physical resources, and overall DTI management, as well as a central management data system operated by HM Treasury;

- to develop additional facilities to increase the scope of the system as users identified needs.

In subsequent years the system evolved to meet the changing needs of its users. A User Requirement Specification was agreed in 1983, and work began on a limited microcomputer-based system (the 'Core' system) for personnel managers, which became operational in January 1984. The PERMIS Extended System was then developed by a team from a U.K. hardware/software company under DTI direction and its first part (which superseded the 'Core' system) entered service in November 1985. In addition to the central staff records system for personnel management staff, it fed information to the DTI's financial, physical resources, and overall management systems. Though generally successful, the system highlighted the need for further development.

Part two of the Extended System was deferred pending the outcome of a comprehensive User Requirement Review (URR). The results of the review (August 1986) set out 37 areas in which PERMIS might usefully be developed further. At this stage the U.K. company left the project and all development work fell to the DTI Project Team.

In subsequent years further modules were introduced and PERMIS software has required constant enhancement and modification to cope with changes of personnel policy and practice. Before each software change, system analysts have examined, where appropriate, existing manual practices to determine the most efficient approach, and a cost/benefit analysis has been undertaken to ensure that expected benefits (quantifiable and unquantifiable) justify the estimated cost of making the change.

Computerisation of personnel records has undoubtedly brought the DTI several advantages compared with a system of paper records:

- PERMIS provides approximately 650 users in management units throughout DTI with a central database of human resource information, and allows multiple access to data (subject to confidentiality and security controls);

- the system reduces the need for individual user groups to keep their own records, and eliminates duplication of data capture on manual or local computer systems;

- data can easily be passed electronically to and from other computer systems within the DTI (to pass information manually, in the same detail and with the same frequency, would be prohibitively expensive);

- data retrieval is easy and PERMIS can be programmed to produce a report of specified staff (e.g. those of a specified age or with specified skills) far more quickly and cheaply than could be done manually. (Thousands of reports are produced annually in this way.)

There have also been disadvantages:

- initially some staff were reluctant to abandon familiar paper records for an unfamiliar computer system (younger and more junior staff adapted most quickly);

- because PERMIS was tailormade for the DTI, the DTI alone had had to bear the entire cost of maintaining and modifying it. Employing specialist systems analysts and programmers has been expensive.

PERMIS is coming to the end of its useful life and the DTI will be seeking a replacement for it. (The form of the replacement is as yet undecided.)

Various organisations now offer ready-made personal computer systems. Since these have not been developed with the DTI's needs in mind, their use might entail loss of flexibility. Nevertheless, it may be possible for the DTI to share the cost of necessary modifications to such a system with other users. Furthermore, such systems usually include simple report-generation facilities, which may help to avoid the delay and expense of employing specialist programmers for this task.

SECTION 2: MAKING GOVERNMENT MORE EFFICIENT

2.1 Establishing an efficiency programme

The United Kingdom's Efficiency Unit, reporting to the Prime Minister's Adviser on Efficiency and Effectiveness, was created in 1979. The role of the Unit is to advise on how to improve the efficiency and effectiveness of central government and to help government departments to improve the value for money of the resource which they use. It does this through an Efficiency Scrutiny programme.

The context for change

Scrutinies have three main aims:

- securing value for money;
- improving quality of service;
- improving managerial and organisational effectiveness.

The Efficiency Unit is also responsible for helping develop the Government's range of public sector reforms, designed to raise the standard of public services and to make them answer better to the wishes of their users, and since 1992 the Unit has had responsibility for co-ordinating market-testing policy and activity.

Implementing change

Throughout its existence, the Unit has combined Civil Service and private sector experience, by drawing its staff from secondees from other government departments and the private sector. There are currently, including support staff, 14 people in the Unit. It is headed by a Civil Service Grade 3, with a Grade 5 deputy. There is one other Grade 5 in the Unit. There are three private sector consultants, at roughly equivalent level, seconded from companies in the private sector, and one exchange officer on loan from the Australian public service. All secondments are for approximately two years. This team is supported by two Grade 7s and five support staff in Personal Secretary and Administrative grades. The Unit has deliberately remained small, with an advisory and monitoring role.

To support the efficiency programme, each Grade 5 or equivalent is allocated a number of government departments and is responsible for overseeing efficiency scrutiny work in that area. The Efficiency Unit member is required to familiarise himself or herself with their departments, and to provide advice and help on techniques for improving value for money. The Unit member will also be involved with departments in their Efficiency Scrutiny programmes. The essence of the Efficiency Unit approach is to act as adviser, to provide support and encouragement to departments, and to monitor departments' progress – but not to usurp the responsibility for activity within departments. The responsibility for using resources in the most cost-effective way properly remains with each government department. The Efficiency Unit does not seek to dilute the responsibility of the Minister or the Accounting Officer in the department, but simply to provide a source of help so that this responsibility can be effectively discharged.

Each department is required to develop an Efficiency Scrutiny programme, with the aims of securing value for money, improving the quality of service and improving managerial and organisational effectiveness. The stages of a scrutiny, and the allocation of responsibilities of a scrutiny are set out in a guide that is given to each scrutiny team.

The scrutiny team is drawn from within the department, but not from the area to be reviewed. After the scrutiny is set up, the investigation phase occupies 90 working days, which are taken up with the drafting of a study plan, collection of evidence and production of emerging findings and completion of the final report. The Efficiency Unit is involved at each stage and the nominated Unit desk officer would aim to spend some time with the team during its work. But it remains the responsibility of the department in question to undertake the scrutiny, decide on the recommendations, prepare the action plan and ensure implementation. The Efficiency Adviser will monitor this activity and comment to the departmental Minister on the success of this process. Since 1979, accumulated savings from scrutinies amounts to more than £1.5 billion and they are currently generating savings of around £100-200 million per year. There have usually been something like 20-25 scrutinies per year. Each scrutiny can cost up to £100,000.

Approximately 350 scrutinies have been undertaken since 1979. Investigations in 1993 covered such issues as customer satisfaction in the Department of Social Security; information needs in the Department for Education; and common causes of error in Customs and Excise. There will now be a shift of emphasis in the efficiency scrutiny programme. Departments are now very familiar with the scrutiny technique and often apply this approach to studies of their own, not formally part of the efficiency scrutiny programme. The Efficiency Unit will continue to encourage departments to work in this way and will concentrate its attention on a somewhat smaller programme of individual departmental scrutinies of areas of high value and high importance. Not every department will necessarily undertake a formal scrutiny every year, therefore, but all departments are aware that they are still expected to contribute to the efficiency scrutiny programme. At the same time the Efficiency Unit will devote more attention to scrutiny of issues which are important across government as a whole. Studies will be undertaken by teams usually seconded to the Efficiency Unit from departments, with private sector involvement if necessary. They will operate to efficiency scrutiny techniques and generally to a normal efficiency scrutiny timetable.

As with every other stage of a scrutiny, implementation responsibility rests with the relevant government department. The appointed Action Manager is responsible for preparing an action plan which must be approved by the departmental Minister and Permanent Secretary. The action manager is also responsible for consulting trade unions and other interested bodies. The action manager ensures that approved recommendations are implemented and prepares a final implementation report within two years. The Efficiency Adviser is involved at each stage of this process, and is able to comment to departmental Ministers on the acceptability of the implementation process. The Efficiency Unit would also expect to be involved, through periodic reports on progress, with the implementation process and will monitor the progress made. This process has been relatively unchanged since it was established in 1979 and the basic methodology has been well tested and is sound. It ensures that action will occur and that change will take place.

A particular initiative in establishing an efficiency programme: an efficiency scrutiny of career management and succession planning in the Civil Service

Many of the scrutinies undertaken by the Efficiency Unit explore issues related to the management of the Civil Service. It is quite usual for a report to consider the current management or organisation of an activity and to recommend that a change of status – perhaps to an Executive Agency or a contractorisation – should be considered. In November 1993 the Efficiency Unit published a *study of career management and succession planning in the Civil Service.* Its terms of reference were:

> "To consider, in the light of the changing structures and job needs of the Civil Service, the policies and practices for ensuring the adequate supply of suitably qualified people able to fill senior posts in both Agencies/Executives and Departmental Headquarters (whether from internal sources or by direct recruitment after Open Competition), and to make recommendations to the Head of the Home Civil Service."

The study was run on efficiency scrutiny lines but, in view of the major and wide-ranging issues under examination, was not constrained by the normal 90 working day timetable for a scrutiny. The main recommendations of the study were:

- the key principles of recruitment through fair and open competition, promotion through merit, the emphasis on integrity, objectivity and impartiality, and non-politicisation continue to remain valid and should be preserved;

- there should be more explicit criteria for selection, appraisal, development and promotion of staff at Grade 3 and above;

- for each appointment at Grade 3 level and above, the case for advertisement – within the department, across the Civil Service or full open competition – should be considered: the result should be monitored and reported in the Cabinet Office departmental report;

- proposals for alternative contracts of employment for the senior open structure (the top three grades) should be developed which would safeguard against politicisation but strike an appropriate balance between risks and rewards: a contract of indefinite term but with a clear, specific period of notice is recommended;

- the Next Steps Project Manager should review the extent to which fixed-term contracts continue to meet the requirements for recruiting appropriate people as Next Steps Agency Chief Executives;

- departments should have more discretion to construct varied compensation packages to encourage some senior staff to leave early.

The Government accepted that the systems of career management and succession planning should be more open and the Prime Minister's statement at the time of publication said:

> "The Civil Service is being restructured with departmental headquarters concentrating on policy making and the purchasing of services which increasingly are provided by Agencies in Government or on contract from the private sector. The systems for recruitment, appointment and career management of civil servants need to be matched to these changing tasks and responsibilities and the skills and qualities needed in the Civil Service in the future. At the same time the Government agrees with the need to preserve an impartial, non-political Civil Service recruited and promoted on merit."

The Government published a White Paper "The Civil Service: Continuity and Change" in July 1994. It accepted the recommendations of the report and made proposals which went significantly further. The main proposals were:

- A new wider senior Civil Service should be created, covering broadly the range of responsibilities currently at Grade 5 and above.

- Each department to review its senior managment structure with a view to reducing layers of management where possible.

- Departments and Agencies to consider advertising openly posts at these levels when appointments are made and should do so whenever necessary to provide a strong field or to introduce new blood.

- Members of the new Senior Civil Service should be on written contracts. One form to be used in the majority of cases – employment for an indefinite term but with specified periods of notice. Fixed-term and rolling contracts to be used as appropriate.

- A new, more flexible pay system for this group, with more pay variation on the basis of wider pay ranges within the overall pay bill.

The White Paper says the Government believes that departments and Agencies should now be given greater freedom and flexibility to develop programmes for improving efficiency which best meet their own needs, with less detailed central oversight. From 1995, departments and Agencies will draw up efficiency plans each Spring, indicating what measures they propose to take to stay within their running cost limits for the coming three years. These will include privatisation, contracting out and market-testing. The Efficiency Unit, in co-operation with the Treasury, will review these plans and discuss with departments where necessary.

In 1992, the Efficiency Unit acquired responsibility from the Treasury for the Market-Testing programme. The Unit is responsible for developing policy on market-testing although the responsibility for developing market-testing programmes rests with individual departments since they are best placed to know their own business and to identify which activities are most appropriate to market-testing. It also acts in an advisory capacity, encouraging departments to examine market-testing possibilities and as a clearing house for best practice to ensure that all Departments are equally aware of the prospects and of the practical considerations that they need to address.

In the White Paper "Competing for Quality", published in November 1991, the Government set out ways to secure better value for money in the public service. It described the development of market-testing as a further technique which could be applied to activities which could benefit from a competitive discipline but where, unlike in privatisation or strategic contracting cases, the Government had not taken a strategic policy decision to put an activity outside government or abolish it, but wished to apply a value for money test. As the Government explained in "Competing for Quality", for a genuine value for money test to be applied, in-house teams should have the opportunity to put forward a firm bid on the same basis and timescale as the private sector. They are encouraged to propose imaginative and radical ways of undertaking the activity.

Market-testing has always been available to departments as one of the techniques which they can use in deciding whether to contract out work to the private sector. Until 1992, however, no more than £25 million of activity was subjected to market-testing across government as a whole. In the Citizen's Charter White Paper published in November 1992, the Government set out plans for a major step change in the level of market testing, and published departmental plans which amounted in total to activities worth £1.5 billion and covering 44,000 posts.

The first year's commitment to market-testing programmes ran until 30 September 1993. In line with the Charter principle of openness, the Government is publishing the results of the first year's programme.

Whilst each U.K. efficiency scrutiny has cost up to £100,000 and the total costs of the programme are therefore in the region of £2 million to £3 million per year, including the direct running costs of the Unit itself, they have generated accumulated savings of £1.5 billion since 1979.

Supporting material

i) Career Management and Succession Planning Study, The Efficiency Unit (November 1993) HMSO, ISBN 0-11-430092-5, £9.95

ii) White Paper "The Civil Service: Continuity and Change" – Cm 2627, HMSO, ISBN 0-10-126272-8, £7.10

2.2 Improving productivity

The U.K. Government's policy aims are:

- to set an overall ceiling for public spending;
- to focus public resources on core activities;
- to use choice, competition and market forces in providing or securing public services;
- to seek maximum value for money from a given input.

Wherever practicable, privatisation – whether into competitive markets or toughly regulated regimes – or the wholesale contracting out of activities are the Government's preferred course, because the private sector offers the greatest scope and greatest incentive to respond to customers' needs.

The Next Steps Initiative, launched in 1988, has an important role in helping to achieve better value for money in the delivery of government services.

A Next Steps Agency is an Executive Unit in a government department. Responsibility for delivery of a service is delegated to the Agency's Chief Executive, who is appointed by the Minister. The Agency must operate within a publicly stated framework, determined by the Minister, covering policy, resources, performance targets, flexibilities and accountability. Within this framework, the Chief Executive has full responsibility in managing the Agency on a day-to-day basis.

Agencies are not set up unless they offer the firm prospect of achieving greater economy, efficiency and effectiveness than under alternative or existing arrangements. Before a decision is taken to set up an Agency, the Government must be satisfied that the activity in question should not be abolished or privatised or contracted out to the private sector. A review of the same options takes place at regular intervals after the launch. Broadly similar arrangements apply to executive non-departmental public bodies.

Around three quarters of civil servants are expected to be working in Next Steps Agencies or bodies operating on Next Steps principles by the mid-1990s.

The Citizen's Charter initiative is also part of a conscious effort to devolve management decisions away from the centre, within a firm framework of control and accountability. There are also considerable overlaps with programmes for improving efficiency and establishing performance measures. The rationale is to benefit the customer and the taxpayer.

The context for change

Where the Government decides that an activity should remain the responsibility of the public sector, it seeks value for money through a variety of mechanisms:

- Setting *aims, objectives, performance indicators* and *targets* for departmental activity within a strategic planning framework for each department. With Treasury encouragement, departments are quantifying their outputs and gearing their efforts to the achievement of published targets and reporting on progress in their departmental reports. The Citizen's Charter underpins these developments by emphasising the high quality of service within affordable resources;

- *Tight control of departmental running costs*, under which departments are required to absorb a significant part of increases in these costs through annual gains in efficiency;

- Regular *market-testing*, to establish which provider – public or private – should be used to deliver a programme or service to the required standard at least cost to the taxpayer. Departments publish annual targets for market-testing;

- The development of *purchaser/provider relationships, internal markets, service level agreements, delegated budgets* and *other market-based flexibilities* within government. An internal market has been introduced in the National Health Service. Customer/contractor relationships within and between departments are being widely developed, as are service level agreements. Agencies are of course also an example of a customer/contractor relationship. The Minister remains the owner of the Agency, but contracts with the Chief Executive to deliver a particular level of service. An increasing number of services are being delivered through trading funds, which permit a commercial type approach to the management of public resources;

- *Closer linking of pay to performance:* pay agreements are increasingly focusing on individual performance, while pay determination is being increasingly delegated, in order that reward may be better tailored to the operational needs of the unit;

- Investment projects are subject to rigorous and systematic *cost-benefit appraisal*. Individual policies and programmes are subject to *evaluation* by departments in rolling timetables. *Efficiency Scrutinies* are conducted both within and across departments, to examine whether current programmes are achieving their objectives, or whether the means for delivering the objectives need revising.

Experience suggests that probably the most vital requirement or precondition for successful action is commitment from the top, preferably from Ministers. Without this, there is a serious risk that the initiative will be overwhelmed by pressure to maintain the status quo.

The Next Steps Initiative, which started in 1988, is targeted for completion by the mid-1990s.

Implementing change

An action plan for launching a Next Steps Agency is a good example of an implementation programme. Broadly, the steps are as follows:

- agree that setting up a Next Steps Agency is the best way of delivering the service concerned (the "Prior Options" exercise, as descibed in the Introduction);

- appoint Chief Executive by open competition;

- agree on the policy and resources framework within which the Agency will operate;

- install suitable management information systems;

- set up suitable performance indicators and targets;

- settle the arrangements for public accountability;

- publish framework document setting out the agreed arrangements for the matters listed above and the demarcation of responsibility between Minister and Chief Executive;

- where appropriate, publish corporate and business plans;

- after launch, periodic reviews to assess whether the Agency is still serving its purpose, or whether one of the other prior options should be adopted at this stage.

Supporting material

"Executive Agencies – A Guide to Setting Targets and Measuring Performance", HMSO, June 1992, ISBN 0-11-560040-x, £3.25

2.3 Market-testing and contracting out services

Market-testing is a process by which government departments assess whether the services for which they are responsible can best be delivered in the public sector or the private sector.

The objective of market-testing is to promote fair and open competition in order to achieve the best value for money for both the customer and the taxpayer. In achieving this objective, there is the need to find the supplier of a particular service (or services) whose combination of quality, price and other relevant factors offers the greatest value for money in the long term. When a market-test shows that better value for money is to be obtained through buying in a service, the Government remains responsible for ensuring that it is managed effectively.

The process of approaching service-providers within the private sector, and their bidding (i.e. responding to a tender) for a particular area of work, is known as contracting out.

Contracting out services can in fact be a prior option to market-testing, i.e. a decision is made for policy reasons that the work should be done in the private sector, **or** it may result from market-testing, i.e. a decision has been made that better value for money can be obtained from the private sector.

Each government department has established a market-testing programme for the year ending September 1993: details appeared in The Citizen's Charter report published in 1992.

In general terms, activities which have been found to be particularly suitable for market-testing are of the following types:

- resource intensive;
- relatively discrete;
- specialist or support services;
- subject to fluctuating work patterns;
- subject to a quickly changing market;
- subject to rapidly changing technology.

The context for change

The White Paper, Competing for Quality, published in 1991 set out the Government's plans to achieve better value for money. In particular by opening up more public services to competition from the private sector, whilst making it clear that the Government had no dogmatic preference for private or public provision of services.

Competing for Quality required government departments and agencies to assess the scope, within the widest possible range of activities, for extending market testing to new areas of their operations and to set targets for activities to be tested by 30 September 1993.

Implementing change

HM Treasury has produced detailed guidance and in accordance with that, each department establishes, usually through a specialised market-testing function, its own approach to undertaking market-testing. Typically, a steering group is formed to oversee the market-test and to ensure that all relevant departmental interests are adequately represented and consulted.

In establishing a market-testing programme, each department needs to review its activities and identify candidates for testing.

It should address the following questions:

- Is the function or activity essential? What are the implications of *not* doing it? Or of doing it in a reduced or combined form elsewhere?

- Can the activity be performed more economically by other means (e.g. a press cuttings service rather than provision of newspapers and journals)?

- What is the full cost of the level of service presently provided and that which is considered necessary? (Costs will include operating costs – staff, supervision and consumables – and overhead costs – accommodation, utilities and management.)

- Is the function or activity organisationally discrete?

- What are the working methods, organisation and use of capital assets? What use is proposed of existing staff and assets?

Managers should consider whether any prior options exist, e.g. should a service cease altogether, be privatised or contracted out for policy reasons.

Managers should take care to identify any interactions of activities proposed for market testing with other activities within the department.

It is essential to obtain commitment to the programme at all levels of management. Once the programme has been agreed, managers should carefully make staff aware of it, observing established consultation procedures.

Having obtained the necessary agreement to the test of a particular area, the first stage is to identify the detailed scope of the services to be tested. The next stage is to define the user-need for the service, and to establish the cost of the existing service. A specification for the service is then drawn up: this will form part of the invitation to tender. The department in question normally encourages the current service providers to submit an in-house bid.

When the tenders are received, they are evaluated in terms of quality, price, reliability, and all other relevant factors, to determine which offers the best overall long-term value for money. Line management, in consultation with departmental ministers as necessary, eventually makes the decision on whether the service should be retained in-house or contracted out.

If the service is retained in-house, then a service level agreement is made with the in-house team. If the service is contracted out, then a contract with the chosen supplier is established.

The time spent in completing a market test will vary according to the complexity of the activity being tested. Most tests take longer than six months, with the average being about nine months.

Any schedule should incorporate timescales for:

- preparation of the specification of the work;
- preparation of the standards of the work;
- drafting legal requirements;
- any necessary management reviews;
- receipt of tenders;
- completion of the bid analysis process;
- award of contract;

- the need to comply with European Community Directives.

In the recently published White Paper "The Civil Service: Continuity and Change", the Government proposes that departments and Agencies should draw up efficiency plans to show how they propose to remain within their running cost limits over the next three years. These plans will include privatisation, contracting out and market-testing. In future, therefore, there will be less central direction in relation to these programmes, although they will continue to be centrally monitored.

The Government has introduced changes in the use of privately raised finance to enable the public and private sectors to work together more effectively, particularly on infrastructure projects. It believes that the further improvement of public services requires the substantial expansion of competition. The aim, therefore, is to find new ways of mobilising the private sector to meet needs which have traditionally been met only by the public sector. Specific measures which provide scope for private finance, announced by the Chancellor of the Exchequer in his 1992 Autumn Statement, include important public services such as housing, British Rail and higher education.

Supporting material

i) White Paper, 'Competing for Quality' Cm 1730 ISBN, 0-10-117302-4, £6.85, 1991

ii) White Paper, "The Civil Service: Continuity and Change" – Cm 2627, HMSO, ISBN 0-10-126272-8, £7.10

2.4 Structure of government

This entry confines itself to the mechanism for making changes to the structure of central government.

In the U.K., structure of government matters are handled by the Office of Public Service and Science, which is incorporated in the Cabinet Office. Activity in this area tends to be patchy, as changes to the overall structure are made on an ad hoc basis and usually as the result of political decisions. The organisational pattern of departments and their varying responsibilities are ultimately a matter for the Prime Minister. The aim must be to ensure a balanced and politically effective administration and to reflect changing political emphasis. Changes in structure are likely to be required as policies change and particularly if administrations change as the result of an Election. The most recent examples of structural change came after the last General Election, with the creation of the Department of National Heritage, the absorption of the Department of Energy into the Department of Trade and Industry, and the creation of the Office of Public Service and Science itself.

The context for change

Recent structural reforms in the U.K. Government can be grouped under several headings:

- The role of government itself, e.g. whether a particular activity should or should not be seen as a function of the state; or whether any overall limit should be set on the size and cost of government;

- The structure of central authorities, i.e. the offices of the Head of State, Prime Minister, Cabinet, Ministry of Finance etc.;

- The numbers and size of other Ministries and the arrangements for distribution of functions and for co-ordination of policy and administration between them;

- The relationship between central government and the functions and powers of local and/or regional government;

- The delegation of executive tasks of government to subordinate and accountable bodies or Agencies;

- The functions and powers of independent authorities responsible for audit and investigation of government, and their relationship to Parliament.

Implementing change

Political considerations aside, ideally the first issue to be considered before embarking upon organisational change is whether the objectives can be more readily achieved by changes in policy, internal changes within departments or improvements in inter-departmental co-ordination.

The rules for creating Agencies provide a good example of this. Agencies are not set up unless they offer the firm prospect of achieving greater economy, efficiency and effectiveness than under alternative or existing arrangements. Before a decision is taken to set up an agency, the Government must be satisfied that the activity in question should not be abolished or privatised or contracted out to the private sector. A review of the same options takes place at regular intervals after the launch. This procedure is known as the "prior options" test.

Experience suggests that where an entirely new department is created, it takes at least five years for the benefits of the re-organisation to come through. Even in a re-organisation as relatively small as the incorporation of the Department of Energy into the Department of Trade and Industry, it took at least one year for all the different traditions of the two departments to be amalgamated.

The following checklist has emerged from recent restructuring exercises:

- ***Will the changes result in a more effective grouping of functions within Departments?***

  It is important to establish which functional inter-relationships appear most clearly to reflect the policy priorities of the Prime Minister and the Government. Are these relationships likely to increase or decrease in importance as a result of general trends in policy? Do the advantages of a change outweigh the disadvantages of breaking existing links?

- ***Will the eventual grouping of functions produce a sensible mix of types of function?***

  Functions may be, for example, regulatory, promotional, productive and so on. Introducing new types of work may bring disproportionately heavy overheads.

- ***What should be the size of departments?***

  This needs to take into account the policy span, indicated in the U.K. roughly by the number of Under Secretary (Grade 3) posts (senior officers responsible for a clear section of policy, for example Consumer Affairs, the Iron and Steel Industry etc.).

- ***How should the support functions be changed?***

  Where possible, each department should control its own finance and personnel functions, though shared arrangements can be useful where a department is split up.

- ***How can loyalties be maintained?***

  Staff should generally move with the functions to ensure continuity, although they should normally be offered the opportunity of returning to their original departments if they wish. There is often a considerable degree of loyalty to the parent department and loss of efficiency may result if this is lightly discarded.

2.5 Work measurement

Work Measurement is the use of techniques to establish how long a trained person should take to complete a defined task at acceptable levels of performance and quality. It was first introduced to the industrial workplace to meet the needs of productivity-based payment schemes but has progressed to be widely used throughout the non-industrial areas. It is a recognised specialism within the field of Management Services and as such requires specialist training. Its purpose is to provide managers with objective and accurate information to help them manage their business efficiently and economically. This information can be used in:

- setting staffing levels;
- use of staff;
- work balancing;
- planning;
- cost and labour budgeting;
- monitoring;
- performance control;
- productivity payment systems.

The context for change

Public sector managers do not operate in an environment dictated by profit, but are primarily driven by the need to improve efficiency and control costs. HM Treasury has set up a central unit to:

- encourage the effective use of work measurement within the Civil Service;
- provide help and advice on the effective use of work measurement, including setting appropriate standards;
- provide and maintain a "centre of professionalism" to work measurement practitioners across departments.

Implementing change

Experience in the U.K. Civil Service suggests that as with all implementations for change, it is essential for senior managers to be committed to the introduction of a Work Measurement initiative. Having gained this commitment, everyone affected by the project should be made fully aware of what is going to happen and how it will affect them.

In planning the approach, the team will be influenced by:

- the commitment and wishes of management;
- the characteristics of the work;
- the need for control and planning information;
- the views of the Trade Unions;
- the Work Measurement expertise available.

The next stage is to get answers to the following:

- What is the nature of the work (production/service)?
- How many different types of work?
- Is there a constant flow of work, or peaks and troughs?
- What levels of customer service are to be provided?
- What levels of monitoring and control are required?

This then allows decisions to be made on:

- How to measure?
- What techniques to use?
- What levels of precision/accuracy are required?
- What parts of the work require different skill levels?
- Can the work be balanced to achieve a smooth flow?
- What level of information is required to monitor and control output?

On completion, a successful Work Measurement-based system should:

- quantify achievement;
- be sensitive to change;

- not consume excessive resources on data collection;
- alert management to remedial action where appropriate.

There is no simple guide to the cost of a Work Measurement project. It will vary according to the purpose of the measurement, the range and difficulty of the work to be measured and the detail and accuracy required. Implementation costs should be viewed against the benefits expected from such an investment. It is widely accepted, both in the commercial world and the public sector, that Work Measurement leads to savings – usually in the area of ten to twenty per cent.

The time involved depends upon the type of project undertaken, the complexity of the area being measured and the degree of accuracy required. A short, sharp and broad measurement of a simple workplace may take only a few weeks. On the other hand, measurement of a large department spread over a large number of offices and intended to provide a detailed and accurate database for a full management and information system may well take more than one year.

Having got commitment to proceed, the stages of any problem-solving are:

- DEFINE – the problem;
- OBTAIN – all the facts relevant to the problem;
- EXAMINE – the facts critically but impartially;
- CONSIDER – the courses open and decide which to follow;
- ACT – on the decision;
- FOLLOW UP – the development.

The detailed stages of Work Measurement are:

- SELECT – the work to be studied;
- RECORD – all information of the job or process;
- EXAMINE – the recorded information and challenge its accuracy;
- DEVELOP – agreed procedures and by applying Work Measurement techniques produce time values;
- IMPLEMENT – new procedures, time values and supporting data capture system;
- MAINTAIN – the time values and their currency following changes.

SECTION 3: IMPROVING THE QUALITY OF SERVICES

3.1 Public reporting

3.2 Introducing a quality management approach

3.3 Establishing a customer orientation

3.4 Ensuring a right of redress

3.5 A particular initiative in setting standards: The Passport Agency

3.6 A particular initative in introducing performance indicators : local government

3.1 Public reporting

Public Reporting is taken to be synonymous with open government – the extent to which governments report to the public at large details of policy, performance and information held.

The context for change

In the U.K., a White Paper, setting out government policy and proposals to increase openness, was published on 15 July 1993. Its proposals included the following:

- A code of practice on the release of government information with policy announcements, and access to information, subject to certain exemptions. Government performance against the Code would be policed by the Ombudsman (Parliamentary Commissioner for Administration), who can report to Parliament if he* agrees with a complaint that the Code has been breached;

- There should be a statutory right of access to health and safety information held by government;

- There should be a statutory right of access, by the subject, to personal records held by government;

- There should be selective introduction of amendments to existing Acts, which prohibit disclosure of information – to insert the test that disclosure would cause actual harm.

The primary reasons for these developments are:

- to improve decision-making;

- to provide greater background information for government decisions;

- to assure the public that key facts are not being concealed.

At the same time, the Government aims to retain confidentiality of sensitive information that they have a duty to protect. The Government is keen to make real advances in openness, as a contribution to a more informed democracy.

*The current post holder is male.

This fits in with increased transparency on performance, through the publication of targets etc, for public services. The Citizen's Charter is also promoting increased openness about the reasons for government decisions taken.

Implementing change

In the U.K., the code of practice envisaged in the July 1993 White Paper came into effect in April 1994. Codes of practice for local government and the National Health Service will follow. The two new statutory rights will require legislation – subject to the availability of Parliamentary Time.

The results of the Code should begin to come through as departments become familiar with procedures and with the sorts of information that can and cannot be released. The Ombudsman will develop "case law" which will make interpretation of the Code of Practice easier.

A basic outline of the method of change in the United Kingdom might be as follows:

- launch policy and invite reactions;
- receive comments during consultation period;
- identify areas of concern over implementation;
- provide guidance material and training for staff who will be dealing with applications and for senior staff who will have to make the more difficult judgements;
- possible attitude training to ensure that more information is released as a matter of course;
- consider publicity material for new schemes of applying for information. Make sure it is in plain language and easily understood;
- monitor take-up and problems.

Supporting material

White Paper on "Open Government", Cm.2290, HMSO, ISBN 0-10-122902-x, £11.00, 1993

3.2 Introducing a quality management approach

Quality Management may be defined as:

> "Continuously meeting the agreed customer requirements throughout the organisation at the right cost. Customer satisfaction every time."

There are many other definitions. But what is essential is to see Quality Management as an on-going process, with no middle or end, continuously striving for excellence, and aiming to get things right, first time, every time. Quality does not necessarily mean an expensive, elaborate or luxurious service. It means a product fit for its purpose, reliable and giving value for money. Quality Management has to be led strongly from the top. Customers are defined not simply as the public, but the person next in line to us, in our own department or a neighbouring one.

The first move towards introducing quality systems as such in the U.K. Government came in February 1985 with the announcement of the "Next Steps" initiative. This emphasised a development in the management of service to the public and set in hand the creation of several Agencies to handle much of the work involving service to the public. There was renewed emphasis on customer service and quality management, identifying the competencies required by staff. They would be increasingly exposed to public accountability and organisations would be much more easily made or broken by the reputations gained by the quality of service of their staff.

The context for change

Quality Management originated in the private sector, particularly in the field of manufacturing, where lapses in quality meant customer complaints, waste of materials and products and increased costs in putting them right. It is much more difficult in the public sector to define a product, particularly in policy areas. The main emphasis within government will be upon those areas where a service is provided to the public. However, policy areas can also participate in quality programmes provided that sufficient thought is given to the matter by the managers concerned.

In general, the public has come to expect higher standards of service and particularly from private businesses. The absence of an easily definable product and of a profit motive, and the relative security of government employment have all been disincentives towards achieving quality in the public sector. However, recent years have seen a noticeable change within the public sector and significant efforts are being made to improve services – to good effect.

The Citizen's Charter initiative has also played its part in emphasising the citizen's right to expect a reasonable level of good service from all public sector employees and has given added weight to the importance of achieving high quality results first time round.

The Charter Mark is an award for excellence in delivering public service. It was first announced in the Citizen's Charter White Paper in July 1991. The first 36 awards given under the scheme were presented by the Prime Minister in 1992. Winners included schools, hospitals, government Agencies, police services etc. The aim of the awards is to promote high standards of information and openness, choice and consultation, courtesy and helpfulness.

Implementing change

As one of the first steps in improving the awareness of customer service and quality, the Cabinet Office proposed a pilot "action learning" project, to be spread over nine months, to enable self-nominated departments and agencies to explore and implement their own strategies and actions in response to the Next Steps emphasis on the delivery of service. The overall aim of this project was to support a small number of pilot projects to improve the quality of customer service with a view to:

- demonstrating for their business the key steps in implementing customer service improvements;
- demonstrating for their business the preconditions to effective customer service training;
- capturing the lessons learned for the benefit of departments and Agencies more widely.

The participating organisations formed a consortium to take forward this work and to maximise the lessons learned in the process. The work was jointly funded by the Training and Development Division of the Cabinet Office and members of the Consortium.

Following this successful initiative, the participating departments went on to introduce quality systems elsewhere in their organisations. Also, other departments and Agencies introduced their own quality systems, either on an independent basis or drawing on the experience of Consortium participants. In some departments, senior managers set aside time to participate in a quality seminar, at which the aims and benefits of quality systems were discussed.

Key elements in establishing quality systems have included the following:

- researching *customers' perception* of service and their degree of satisfaction with it;

- the need to establish *measures* of quality of service which then enable one to set realistic *standards* derived from customers' priorities;

- measuring the effective *delivery* of the service;

- once standards are reached, setting *higher standards* for the organisation to achieve reviewing the setting of higher standards for the organisation to achieve;

- continually *monitoring satisfaction* and dealing with any problems that cause the levels to drop.

Quality Management is closely related to a number of other topics. Apart from the "Next Steps Initiative" and the Citizen's Charter there are links with:

- ***Human Resource Management***
  Leadership and team-building are particularly important. There needs to be support and commitment to the initiative from the very top. Staff need to be enthused with a vision of the whole organisation and its purpose as well as the concept of giving a service from one's own area. In organisations embarking on customer service and quality initiatives, the role of the manager was likely to change to one of facilitator, coach and counsellor.

- ***Training and Development***
  Management and leadership training are important to ensure that quality principles are fully understood at all levels of management. There is much to be gained by those who have experienced a quality programme sharing with those who are coming to it afresh. Concepts such as customer care and providing a service need to be very thoroughly put over to staff and explained.

- ***Performance Management***
  There needs to be an emphasis on quality within performance management so that the contribution of individual staff is recognised and monitored. Outputs need to be specified and measured.

- ***Organisational Change***
  Quality systems may often lead to flatter pyramids within organisations and there can be a substantial element of change if long-established proceduresare to be made more efficient. There should be reward systems for staff empowered to take decisions at lower levels.

- ***Workforce Reductions***
  The improved results available through quality systems may possibly, but not necessarily, lead to a reduction in the manpower necessary to achieve the desired results.

For a quality initiative to be successful it is important to:

- establish a baseline from which to review progress;

- define quality for the organisation;

- identify the objectives and priorities of the organisation and of its customers (Customers are not just the public, but all individuals and organisations with whom there are dealings);

- ask customers what their needs are (the organisation may not be able to deliver what they want) in establishing the perception of levels of service provided;

- involve people at all levels: senior managers' commitment is crucial, but staff must also be involved;

- ask for help: those who have introduced quality already will be pleased to assist and encourage, but the help of professional external consultants and facilitators will probably also be needed to introduce a quality programme properly;

- a quality initiative should be ongoing, with the organisation continually striving to excel.

Costs will vary according to the scale of the project. Inevitably, there will be the cost of training to introduce managers to the quality concept and of providing them with back-up reading or video materials. There will be costs in lost productive time as staff are introduced to the quality initiative and attempt to put it into effect, but these should be largely cancelled out by more efficient and more productive working methods in the future. There will also be the cost of surveys of customer needs and ultimately of customer perception of the level of improvement.

Additional record-keeping will be necessary in order to monitor performance carefully and analyse the results against various criteria.

Skills primarily involve managers who are prepared to commit themselves seriously to the quality initiative. Top management commitment must be unswerving and must be maintained over a long period of time. Those best equipped to lead quality initiatives at all levels will be enthusiasts with a vision for true customer service, rather than those who are defensive or prefer to maintain the status quo. It is important to involve staff in the change process and not impose it on them.

Key *stakeholders* include top management and managers at all levels. A quality initiative will often have one key manager appointed to ensure that it stays on course.

Obstacles largely centre on inertia, especially in middle management, and difficulties in persuading staff of the true concept of giving a service. Some will still feel that they are entitled to their job as of right and will hotly defend any attempt to change it.

Generally a one- to two-year period is needed to introduce a proper quality initiative in any organisation. During this period, it should be possible to change staff attitudes if necessary, to determine objectives and customers' requirements and to set some sort of system in train. However, it may well take a further two to three years before the quality system has bedded down and is yielding its full benefits.

Supporting material

With HMSO into TQM – Her Majesty's Stationery Office, from HMSO Publicity (PU23), St Crispins, Duke Street, Norwich NR3 1PD

3.3 Establishing a customer orientation

The United Kingdom Government has made the customer-orientation of public services a priority through the Citizen's Charter, launched by the Prime Minister in July 1991. The Charter is a ten-year programme of radical reform to raise the standards of public service and make them more responsive to their users. Because of the very wide coverage of the Citizen's Charter, this entry cannot be exhaustive, but highlights some of the main elements of the Government's programme.

There are six principles which the Government believes should underlie all public services:

- ***Standards***
  Setting, monitoring and publishing explicit standards for the services that individual users can reasonably expect. Publishing actual performance against these standards.

- ***Information and Openness***
  Full, accurate information readily available in plain language about how services are run, what they cost, how well they perform and who is in charge.

- ***Choice and Consultation***
  The public sector should provide choice wherever practicable. There should be regular and systematic consultation with those who use services. Users' views about services, and their priorities for improving them, should be taken into account in final decisions on standards.

- ***Courtesy and Helpfulness***
  Courteous and helpful service from public servants, who will normally wear name badges. Services available equally to all who are entitled to them and run to suit their convenience.

- ***Putting Things Right***
  If things go wrong, an apology, a full explanation and a swift and effective remedy. Well publicised and easy-to-use complaints procedures, with an independent review wherever possible.

- ***Value for Money***
  Efficient and economical delivery of public services within the resources that the nation can afford. Independent validation of performance against standards.

The context for change

The Government believes that the citizen should be able to count on good public services and that taxpayers have the right to expect that the money they provide is spent to optimum effect. Limited resources to fund services were also a key factor. The Government believes that consumers of public services are entitled to the same high standards of service that the best private sector organisations provide. But if services are to be delivered more efficiently within available resources, there have to be changes and improvements.

Improved standards of service can only be delivered if structures, systems and attitudes within public services are focused on results. Alongside the Charter is a huge programme of managerial change aimed at making public services fitter and readier to deliver what is wanted.

The Citizen's Charter is a ten-year programme, but already there are significant developments. There are now 38 published individual Charters, covering some of the main public services. Others will follow. This means that in these areas the public now has – often for the first time – published standards of service, information on performance, complaints procedures and ways to obtain redress. The Charters will be reviewed and improved year by year. Among the Charters in operation at the moment are:

- Patient's Charter;
- Parent's Charter;
- British Rail Passenger's Charter;
- Courts' Charter;
- Benefits Agency Customer Charter;
- Job Seeker's Charter;
- Taxpayer's Charter;
- London Underground's Customer Charter;
- Child Support Agency Charter.

Through these and other Charters, the citizen can increasingly put pressure on those responsible for providing services to deliver them to the promised standard, rather as commercial competition puts consumer pressure on the performance of private firms. In some cases, new laws have been passed, for example to make sure that Citizen's Charter principles are applied to the privatised utilities, that comparative information about local authority performance is published, and to strengthen inspection arrangements in schools.

Implementing change

The Citizen's Charter is beginning to bring about a marked improvement in service to the public in many areas. For example, the original two-year maximum waiting time for hospital operations has now been reduced to 18 months. Public services accept that their performance is under scrutiny and the Citizen's Charter has a nationally accepted high profile. Whilst in many cases in the past there were pockets of excellence within the public service, all services are now expected to strive to achieve the standards of the best.

One of the most critical requirements is for unswerving, long-term commitment to the concept of customer service. The United Kingdom's Citizen's Charter had Prime Ministerial backing from the outset and even then needed to be regularly re-energised from time to time to keep it in the public eye and to maintain the pressure on service providers to keep up the momentum. The Charter principles are based on common sense and reasonable customer expectations but nevertheless there is a tendency in any large organisation for such worthy aims gradually to lose impact unless there is determined pressure to keep them alive.

Essential to success is the commitment and enthusiasm of those on the 'front line' who have to deliver the improvements. At any level of resources efficiency and effectiveness can improve the quality of what is delivered. The Citizen's Charter programme is in that sense resource-neutral. It involves reorientating and reprioritising existing resources, not the injection of new sums of government money.

Key stakeholders include senior Ministers, Chief Executives and officials in the organisations and departments concerned. However, at the end of the day, it is the individual local official providing the service upon whose performance everything else depends. He or she is the key player.

The U.K. introduced the Citizen's Charter in 1991 and many individual Charters were up and running within one or two years. The Citizen's Charter programme is, however, intended to run for ten years, during which there will be many further developments and improvements.

Supporting material

(i) The Citizen's Charter, HMSO CM 1599, ISBN 0-10-115992-7, £8.50, 1991

(ii) The Citizen's Charter, First Report, HMSO CM 2101, ISBN 0-10-121012-4, £8.50, 1992

(iii) The Citizen's Charter, Second Report, HMSO CM 2540, ISBN 0-10-125402-4, £12.50, 1994

3.4 Ensuring a right of redress

Public sector bodies have always had complaints handling procedures of some type or another, but they have not always had a high profile, nor have they been particularly user-friendly.

The U.K. Government introduced the Citizen's Charter in 1991, with a view to improving all aspects of public service to individuals. One of the aspects particularly addressed by individual departments and organisations was improving the mechanism under which customers could register complaints and obtain redress.

The context for change

The Government is concerned that complaints procedures should be well publicised and easy to use. They are also anxious to ensure that all public services act swiftly and effectively when standards are not met or when things go wrong. Moreover, research has shown that people that wish to find out about public services or make a complaint often do not know how or where to start. They may approach MPs, Ministers and departments, whereas better help might be given by the service itself. People need someone to give them information quickly and reliably about where to go and whom to contact to get their enquiry or problem resolved. This led to the introduction of Charterline.

An effective complaints and redress procedure is seen as essential to making the public service, including local authorities, more responsive to customer needs.

Implementing change

Good complaints systems should be:

- *effective*, aimed at solving the problem and providing at the very least a satisfactory explanation, an apology or some form of redress;
- *readily accessible* to users of services;
- *simple to operate*, with clearly set out procedures and responsibilities;
- *speedy*, with time limits for dealing with complaints;

- *objective*, with provision for an independent means to investigate complaints if necessary;
- *confidential* – people's privacy should be protected;
- *integrated* with the organisation's management information systems.

The Government also intends to set up a Complaints Task Force to look at whether public services' complaint handling is in line with these principles. The Task Force will advise on setting up and improving complaints systems. It will also, if appropriate, identify whether more is needed in the longer term to provide more satisfactory ways of resolving individuals' problems with public services.

The Government is piloting a telephone helpline – "Charterline" – to help people who find it daunting or frustrating to get information from large bureaucracies. Charterline is an advice and information service. It gives:

- information about the Citizen's Charter and about the other charters and statements of charter standards that have been published;
- contact numbers to help people find out more about public services;
- contact numbers for making complaints about services.

If the pilot is successful, Charterline will eventually cover all public services nationwide.

Where internal complaints procedures fail, there must be an external route for taking things further. On behalf of the citizen, Ombudsmen already deal with complaints of alleged injustice caused by maladministration by central government, the National Health Service (NHS) and local authorities. Individuals may approach the Ombudsmen through their Member of Parliament if other attempts at redress have failed.

The essential aim is that the redress procedure should be well publicised and easy to use. Steps to achieve this include:

- review existing complaints machinery;
- research customer perception of existing system;
- analyse areas for improvement;

- encourage participating departments and organisations to propose ways of improving their redress facilities;

- departments etc. launch improved system;

- review operation of system after agreed period and make improvements;

- publish results of redress procedure, highlighting successes and undertaking to deal with weaknesses.

Costs are impossible to predict. They will naturally depend on the volume of complaints and the ease with which they can be dealt with. Almost certainly, however, addressing and dealing with complaints will lead to fewer errors in the future and an improved level of service which will more than compensate for the cost of running the redress procedure.

As far as skills are concerned, staff engaged in complaints procedures clearly need to be tactful and helpful in their dealings with the public. This may well take some degree of training, on (readily available) specialist customer-care courses, which itself will be an expense initially. The Government considers that the investment will however be amply repaid.

Stakeholders include Chief Executives of Agencies, heads of departments and organisations but in particular the individuals responsible for handling the day-to-day complaints. It is upon these individuals that the perceived image of the organisation rest.

3.5 A particular initiative in setting standards: The Passport Agency

This entry focuses on one organisation – the United Kingdom Passport Agency – as an example of an area in which stringent and demanding standards have been set and where they have been met with conspicuous success.

The Passport Agency (formerly called the Passport Office) issues over three and a half million (new, renewed and amended) passports per year to U.K. citizens and handles many thousands of enquiries. Traditionally, it was an area of the Civil Service that was criticised for its slow and uncommunicative service and a somewhat remote and austere image. Since 1988, when the service was computerised, and particularly since Agency status in April 1991, the service has been transformed. The result is that customers now receive passports within a maximum of 20 working days and a number of other important standards are publicised and in general attained.

The context for change

The Agency's major objective is to provide the best possible service for all of its customers. In practice, this means providing a fast and efficient passport service, which takes account of varying customer needs. Considerable efforts have been made to improve the quality of service provided and this was recognised in 1992 with the award of a Charter Mark. This has proved a considerable impetus to the programme of customer service.

Implementing change

The Passport Agency has two key targets:

- a customer service target;
- a financial target.

Both of these are agreed by Ministers, are reviewed annually and are set out in the Corporate and Business Plans.

The key customer service target is to process straightforward, properly completed passport applications within specific periods of time. In 1993-94 the target is to process these applications within a maximum of 20 working days in the period of peak demand between January and June; 15 working days in July and August; and 10 working days at other times of the year.

The key financial target is to reduce costs in real terms and for 1993-94 this relates to a reduction of three per cent in the overall cash operating unit cost, compared with the previous year's outturn. The Agency also has targets for dealing with correspondence and for waiting time for personal callers in all of the Passport Offices, of which there are six in the United Kingdom.

Performance against targets is monitored continually through internal management reports derived from the Agency's financial and management information system. These reports are reviewed regularly by the Director of Operations, in association with managers of individual passport offices. The Agency also conducts regular surveys of customer opinion – over 54,000 customer survey questionnaires have been issued since 1991 – with the return showing a very high level of satisfaction with the service provided. Individual passport offices also hold local customer surveys about the quality of service provided for personal callers.

Aside from the formal targets, the Agency has made great strides to improve its service to the public, in accordance with the principles of the Citizen's Charter. In particular, name badges have been introduced for all staff who meet the public in the course of their work, and standard clothing will be offered for those staff working on the public counters from early next year. Considerable improvements have also been made to the reception and other facilities for the public over the last two years to ensure that customers are inconvenienced as little as possible. Special facilities have been established as part of the Agency's commitment to meet the needs of customers with disabilities.

Comprehensive customer-care training has also been provided for staff who have regular face-to-face contact with the public. Priority is now being given to improving the telephone enquiry service and a number of other major initiatives are taking place with the aim of speeding up the handling of customer enquiries.

A pre-requisite for the success of the Agency has been the development of its service to staff. It has devolved personnel management responsibilities to regional offices. Training officers have been appointed in each office to oversee and expand the programme of staff training and to encourage staff to make the most of the training opportunities. In particular, with the help of consultants, they have run a series of courses in each office to help managers with production line management techniques. Communications with staff have also been greatly improved, with the establishment of a very successful Agency house journal and the introduction in December 1992 of a comprehensive team briefing system. Industrial relations have improved markedly since Agency status, being centred on the Passport Agency

Whitley Committee and its three sub-committees on accommodation, personnel and equal opportunities.

A considerable amount has already been achieved, and further developments are planned to improve management and customer service. This includes developing an effective complaints procedure for the public and establishing a consultative panel of passport users, including the travel trade. The Agency is continuing to make efforts to even out passport demand – the demand in the autumn and winter months being considerably less than that in the remainder of the year. These developments are part of the policy of trying to ensure maximum use of staff time.

The Agency make continuous efforts to monitor and improve management at both senior and local level. As part of this process, regular monthly meetings are held between the Director of Operations and regional managers. Adjustments have also been made within staff complements with the appointment of an operations manager within each office to ensure that the Agency's targets and standards are met.

The clear prerequisite must be a commitment and determination to set and raise standards and to improve the service until those standards are met or exceeded. It is necessary to decide at an early stage which targets are the most important. The Passport Agency addressed the following areas:

- service to customers – by post;
- service to customers – by phone;
- service of customers – personal visits;
- customer satisfaction;
- detecting passport fraud;
- wastage;
- efficiency (passports per staff member);
- financial performance.

In all these areas, the Agency has set targets which are set out in the 1993 Corporate Plan.

Skills necessary to bring about this change naturally involve the clear and unswerving commitment of the Chief Executive and his management team. They are among the key stakeholders in the operation, but so are the staff who carry out the day-to-day operations. It is clearly important for everyone within the organisation to be enthused about and committed to delivering the highest standard of service to the public.

Turning round the Passport Agency's service has taken some five years. The Agency's timescale for making significant demonstrable progress is ongoing and it is certainly its intention to make further improvements in the years ahead.

The success of the Passport Agency in reaching the standards that it has set itself results from the close attention given to management matters and the service provided to both customers and staff.

3.6 A particular initiative in introducing performance indicators: local government

This entry focuses on the arrangements devised by the Audit Commission for comparing the performance of local authorities in England, Wales and Scotland under the Citizen's Charter "Performance Indicators" legislation. The Audit Commission is the body which audits Local Authorities and Health Authorities. Its remit covers only England and Wales; the Scottish Accounts Commission has similar powers in Scotland but have produced a different set of indicators. This entry concentrates on experience in England and Wales.

The first Citizen's Charter White Paper "Raising the Standard" included a commitment to publish league tables of performance for local authorities. This became enshrined in the Local Government Act 1992, which empowered the Audit Commission to require local authorities to publish information on standards of performance achieved over a range of indicators. In the current financial year, there are 77 indicators in all. In future years, more may be added to the list.

The Audit Commission first consulted with groups of citizens, and carried out extensive consumer research into which areas of local authority services most concerned them. They then met with groups of consumer representatives, professional experts and local authority representatives to develop indicators which were meaningful, which were practicable to measure, and which would enable comparisons to be made between different authorities, and over time.

The indicators are published in December each year, and authorities must start collecting the information the following April. This gives authorities time to set up the necessary systems for gathering the information required.

Authorities then measure their performance against the indicators during the financial year, before publishing the results in a local newspaper. The Audit Commission will then publish the results nationally.

The context for change

The keystone of the Citizen's Charter is the need for an informed public. Without meaningful, yet simple, information about the quality of our public services, we cannot expect citizens to make informed judgements about the choice of either individual services or the service providers themselves. By publishing national comparisons of local government performance, the standards which the best local authorities have attained will set a benchmark to which others can aspire. Poor performers will be forced, both internally and by citizens, to improve the quality of their services to the Charter Standard.

In most cases, the performance of local authorities is being measured against locally determined targets. The Government does not see it as its function to set national targets of performance centrally, but instead to provide a consistent measure of performance to enable local residents to make informed decisions about the effectiveness and efficiency of their own local authority.

Implementing change

The first steps were for the Audit Commission to consult with citizens to find out which areas of local authority services interest/concern them and for local authorities to ensure that appropriate systems are in place to collect the information required.

Information was collected by local authorities during 1993-94 and will be published in local newspapers, probably in early 1995. This is a rolling programme, enabling citizens to judge performance over time. After the local information has been published, the Audit Commission will publish national comparisons of performance, so that citizens will be able to compare the performance of their own Council against others of a similar type or background. External pressure from citizens for local authorities to raise their standards of service delivery may not be achieved for some years to come. However, early evidence suggests that local government in general is reacting favourably to the discipline of the Citizen's Charter and the Commission's performance indicators. Local authorities are examining their managerial procedures and practices, and are making their services more responsive to the real needs of the local community.

Supporting material

Citizen's Charter Indicators, "Charting a Course", Audit Commission, HMSO 1992, ISBN 0-11-886093, £6.00

SECTION 4: IMPROVING PARTNERSHIPS WITH ORGANISATIONS/ AGENCIES OUTSIDE CENTRAL GOVERNMENT

4.1 Contestable policy advice

4.2 Deregulation

4.3 Intergovernmental restructuring

4.4 Developing partnerships with academic institutions

4.5 Developing partnerships with industry

4.6 A particular initiative in local empowerment: Inner City Task Forces

4.7 Decentralisation

4.1 Contestable policy advice

There have been suggestions that the provision of policy advice in the U.K. should be put on the same customer/contractor basis that now applies to service delivery through Next Steps Agencies. The Treasury and Civil Service Committee of the House of Commons recently examined this topic and heard suggestions from some quarters that senior officials should be employed on fixed-term contracts, with a clear remit related to producing answers on policy issues. However, this is not the case at the moment. Under the present system, most policy proposals still originate from Ministers and/or those civil servants who are specially designated to produce policy advice. Political advisers play a part in this process and the Prime Minister's office has its own advisers in the form of the No.10 Policy Unit.

This unit is headed by an officer of Deputy Secretary level who is in charge of a team of eight people producing ideas on domestic, economic and foreign affairs for the Prime Minister. Proposals produced by the group are naturally available direct to the Prime Minister who has the opportunity to discuss the topics at a regular weekly meeting, and at other times as necessary, for instance at Cabinet Committees or bilateral meetings with other Ministers. There is little public information available about the Policy Unit, but it will also no doubt consider material submitted unsolicited to the Prime Minister by independent think tanks, pressure groups and academia.

4.2 Deregulation

The Deregulation Initiative, dates back to 1985 but was relaunched at the Conservative Party Conference in 1992 when the Prime Minister declared his personal commitment to deregulation.

It has three key targets or objectives:

i) better existing regulation, to be achieved by cutting unnecessary burdens on business and streamlining existing requirement;

ii) better new regulation (including EC legislation), to be achieved by introducing new requirements only where necessary, minimising costs of compliance and consulting business about changes;

iii) better enforcement of regulation, to be achieved by ensuring that local authorities and national inspectorates apply regulations consistently and provide simple and accessible guidance to make it easier for business to comply.

The context for change

The Deregulation Initiative aims to cut "red tape" (from Whitehall, the town hall and Brussels), which stops businesses from getting on with their primary task of producing goods and services. It is particularly concerned with smaller businesses, which are disproportionately affected by over-regulation and face the difficulty of making their voice heard by government. It therefore aims to reduce significantly administrative and regulatory burdens on business. The U.K. Government believes that business enterprise was often being stifled by too much government intervention in economic activity. This risks discouraging innovation and removing incentives. The aim is to do away with some of the costs, delays and uncertainties in business caused by unnecessary government bureaucracy. A significant point is that the impact on business is cumulative, so that even fairly minor requirements when added together represent a significant burden.

Implementing change

The main elements of the programme are:

- The Deregulation and Contracting Out Bill which is currently before Parliament. It effects a number of deregulatory changes to primary legislation and provides a new mechanism to make changes in the future in appropriate cases, subject to public consultation and Parliamentary scrutiny.

- The setting up of a new Deregulation Task Force to succeed the earlier Task Forces. The seven original Task Forces of businessmen appointed in 1993 made over 600 proposals for deregulation of which 359 have now been accepted.

- An eighth Task Force on Charities and the Voluntary Sector is due to report soon.

- Compliance cost assessments for new legislation required to be published. This involves a detailed look at any new legislation to see what would be the cost of businesses putting it into practice.

- Scrutiny of how U.K. has implemented EC legislation. There have been suggestions that some legislation has been implemented too tightly and legalistically.

- Publication by the EC of its legislative programme, indicating those proposals to be subject to an impact assessment.

- Local authority/business partnerships set up to provide guidance to business on how regulations apply to them.

- Two reviews to examine how to remove duplication in the work of local government enforcement agencies and fire safety. These have both now submitted reports to government which is considering their recommendations. The Fire Safety Report was published on 22 June 1994.

- Following the Prime Minister's announcement of a new drive on deregulation in 1992, all government departments were asked to review *all* their regulations to identify candidates for repeal or simplification. The President of the Board of Trade has now reported on the results of the Reviews to the Prime Minister. As a result of this work and also the work by the business task forces, there are now over 870 regulations earmarked for amendment or repeal.

The Deregulation Bill is expected to deal with those changes requiring primary legislation and the Deregulation Task Force in conjunction with departments will continue the offensive against over-regulation by identifying further candidates for repeal or reform. To ensure that over-regulation does not become a problem in the future, all proposals for new regulation are now accompanied on publication by an assessment of the costs to business.

The Deregulation Initiative also affects local authorities. There are now 20 local authority business partnerships which were first launched on 30 June 1992 in several representative pilot areas. They are giving business clear and simple guidance on how regulations apply to them and on services provided by local authorities. The Deregulation Unit is encouraging inspectors and enforcement agencies to learn to distinguish between companies deliberately trying to evade controls and a vast majority trying to abide by the law but sometimes finding the task of achieving more difficult than it should be.

Deregulation starts from a clear conviction that businesses should be restricted as little as possible by legislation. There does of course need to be a clear balance between deregulation and a free-for-all in which adequate safety and consumer safeguards are not in place. One of the main emphases of deregulation in the U.K. has been the elimination of restrictions that were at best trivial and probably unnecessary (for example, a long-standing requirement in law to clean factory walls at particular intervals, rather than when commonsense dictated it).

This is a Ministerial initiative and the key stakeholders are the Deregulation Ministers in each deregulatory department who are in turn responsible to their Secretaries of State and the Prime Minister. Each department has its own Departmental Deregulation Unit which is responsible for ensuring that the Deregulation Initiative is carried out within that department and reports regularly to the Deregulation Minister.

4.3 Intergovernmental restructuring

The powers of local authorities in the U.K. are set out in a number of statutes which have been enacted by Parliament over the years. The Government firmly believes that Parliament should make conscious decisions about which activities and responsibilities are assigned to local government.

Unlike many of their European counterparts, U.K. authorities do not enjoy a power of general competence (although they have an important discretionary power to undertake other activities which they believe to be in the interests of local citizens under Section 137 of the Local Government Act 1972). The introduction of such a power would require major ongoing legislation to define what local authorities may not do. The assumption that where this power exists they have a freer hand can be misleading, since where this is the case there is usually an extensive raft of legislation setting out precisely what they are prevented from doing.

There have been many ebbs and flows of local government functions over the years. Although local government has lost certain responsibilities since 1979, there have also been gains – in particular, the administration of housing benefit was transferred from the Department of Health and Social Security (DHSS) to local authorities in 1982, the discretion to grant non-domestic rates rebates to charities or to ratepayers sustaining hardship was transferred in 1988 and, as a result of the community care reforms, local government has been given lead responsibility for assessing people's needs in this area.

The key reforms in this area have been:

- To introduce a "National Non-Domestic Rate" (NNDR), set at a uniform rate in the pound for all business and other non-domestic premises in England, the total sum collected being re-distributed to local authorities on a per capita basis. The NNDR replaced locally variable business rates.

- To replace local domestic rates/community charges with a Council Tax on each domestic property, based on the relative value of properties (each being placed in one of eight valuation bands, covering a range of values) with discounts for smaller households.

- To allocate central government support for local government services between authorities on the basis of "Standard Spending Assessments" (SSAs) for each authority. SSAs are based on indicators (e.g. the number of school pupils) which allow the relative spending needs of authorities to be assessed. They also take account of the capital Government's view of the appropriate amount of expenditure for local authorities as a whole.

Grant is distributed in such a way that every authority in England should be able to set the same value of Council Tax for properties in a particular valuation band, if they spend at the level of their "SSA".

- To introduce "capping" of local authority budgets, allowing the Secretary of State to designate an authority which, in his view, has set a budget which is excessive, or has increased its budget by an excessive amount, according to general criteria determined by him, and to set a limit on the size of that budget, with which the authority must comply.

- To increase central funding for local authority expenditure, resulting in a reduction in the proportion met from local domestic taxation from 28 per cent in 1990/91 to 16 per cent in 1993/94.

The main objectives of the reforms have been to:

- place local authority revenue finance on a surer footing, improving the transparency of the system and increasing local accountability;

- distribute the burden of local taxation more firmly;

- exercise firmer control over the level of local government revenue expenditure, as part of the control of public expenditure as a whole;

- protect local taxpayers – domestic and non-domestic – from excessive levels of local taxation.

The context for change

Against a background of rapid change, a key issue is the degree of trust between local and central government. Following a speech in 1990 by the then Secretary of State Michael Heseltine, the Government has tried to bridge the gulf of misunderstanding that has existed between itself and local authorities.

The Secretary of State and other Ministers meet the Chairmen of the local authority associations regularly to discuss current concerns, whilst the Permanent Secretary maintains regular contact with the associations at official level.

Implementing change

This section describes two specific measures being taken to improve relations between central and local government:

(i) The Secondments Initiative Programme (SIP);

(ii) Local Government Seminars.

The Secondments Initiative Programme (SIP) is designed to encourage and enable civil servants and local authority executives to exchange posts for periods of up to two years. The Programme is aimed principally at staff in generalist policy and management positions. Although intended primarily for civil servants in Grades 7-5 and their local government equivalents, the programme is open to staff of all grades and ages with appropriate experience or potential, and with clear prospects of further promotion.

It is intended that SIP will increase understanding and co-operation between the two spheres and will encourage the cross-fertilisation of fresh ideas and new ways of thinking. High quality officers from local government obtain first hand experience of policy formation whilst civil servants experience service provision at the sharp end where it impacts on people's lives.

A target of achieving 140 secondments over three years was set at the launch of SIP, but it is intended that the Programme will continue indefinitely.

No legislation was required to implement the Programme. SIP was given a public launch by Ministers and local government leaders. Continuing widespread publicity has been maintained by leafleting and articles in the specialist press. Officers interested in the scheme apply to their personnel offices or directly to the Local Government Management Board who arrange details of each secondment with the organisations involved. A number of seminars have been arranged for secondees to enable them to share their experiences with colleagues.

It was immediately apparent that the most important prerequisites for success were to ensure that as many central and local government staff as possible were aware of the Programme and to guarantee that their applications or expressions of interest would be properly dealt with.

Secondments should not have major cost implications for either of the authorities involved – the usual practice is for a secondee to continue to be paid by his/her parent organisation, but for these costs to be reimbursed by the receiving employer.

Other minor cost implications obviously arise from the staff time involved in administering the scheme, but most of the administration involved is carried out by the Local Government Management Board.

The progress of the Programme has been closely monitored at a number of levels. The Permanent Secretaries of the departments involved meet every six months to discuss progress. Day to day monitoring is carried out by the Department of the Environment's Personnel and Local Government directorates.

The 24-hour *Local Government Seminars* are held annually at the Civil Service College, Sunningdale. Approximately 35 participants attend, split equally between the permanent secretaries of the home government departments and local authority representatives, mainly Chief Executives, but also directors of departments. The programme allows for discussion of a variety of topics of interest to both sides.

The object of the seminars is to improve links and understanding at a senior level between central and local government.

It is intended that the seminars will continue on an annual basis for the foreseeable future. They have already made an important contribution to improved central-local government relations.

The seminars are organised by the Local Government Directorate of the Department of the Environment in close liaison with the Civil Service College who have much experience of organising such events. The cost to the Department of organising the seminars is minimal, as each individual's accommodation costs are met by his/her own organisation. The lessons learnt from each seminar are valuable in preparing for the next occasion.

The first preparations for a seminar begin soon after the preceding one has been concluded. Early consideration is given to the individuals to be invited, the nature of the discussions and who should lead them, and deciding on a guest speaker. Potential local government attendees are chosen largely according to the contribution it is thought that they can make to discussion. A balance is struck between those who have attended in previous years and new attendees. As the seminar approaches, attention is focused on preparing papers for the discussions and on more practical considerations, such as travel arrangements and menus.

4.4 Developing partnerships with academic institutions

There is a wide variety of partnerships with academic institutions that exist across the whole of U.K. Government. The arrangements differ according to the nature of the work of the particular department. This section indicates some of the main areas of interchange between government and academic institutions but concentrates on one example of such partnerships set up by the Department of Trade and Industry as part of the "Managing in the 90s" programme.

The context for change

There is mutual advantage from the partnership between academic institutions and government departments. Academic institutions are an important source of advice in the development of policy and management practice. They may provide:

- proposals for policy development;
- experts for advisory committees;
- a sounding board for policy proposals – offering new ideas and broader perspectives;
- a research capacity;
- consultants to examine particular aspects of policy, administration or management;
- training in public management or in particular specialisms, e.g. personnel management and internal audit training.

Work for the public sector provides an important source of income for academics, through research contracts, consultancy fees and fees for attendance at committees, etc. It also provides access to practical examples of policy implementation and outcomes against which to test the theoretical background. There is benefit from interchange of personnel with secondments of academic staff into government and vice versa.

Good relations with universities are cultivated through an arrangement whereby the Permanent Secretaries of departments each have links with two universities which they take an interest in and visit from time to time.

Universities also provide an important recruiting ground for staff at Executive Officer level and for the fast stream schemes. The office of the Civil Service Commissioner organises programmes of "Graduates in Government" (GiG) Careers Information Fair which enable staff working in departments and agencies to provide details of their work and opportunities to students in a cost-effective way. Commissioners also have a programme of visits each year to Institutes of Higher Education and links with the Association of Graduate Careers Advisory Services (AGCAS).

A particular initiative in developing partnerships with academic institutions: "Managing in the 90s" (Department of Trade and Industry)

"Managing in the 90s" is intended to improve management practice in British businesses, rather than within the Civil Service itself. However, the techniques used would be similar if the exercise were directed at the public sector, and relationships would need to be developed with academic institutions and other knowledgeable bodies. It is an awareness programme designed to help managers in British companies respond to change, to adapt, to innovate and to plan for continuous improvements. In other words, to introduce best practice into all their activities. The programme provides seminars, workshops, literature, videos etc, and signposts managers to further sources of help.

Academic institutions have provided much of the input to the programme and have helped prepare the content of the printed materials which the Department of Trade and Industry (DTI) issues to industry. They have also organised a variety of seminars and events for businessmen. DTI have a range of contacts across the country's business schools and with individual academics so that fresh material and revisions to existing material can be prepared quickly to respond to current needs.

In order for companies to compete successfully with the leaders in their respective fields, there is a need to develop world-class abilities. The commercial sector does not fill the gaps, particularly in respect of smaller and medium-sized firms. Competitive advantage depends increasingly on the effective management of change across wide areas of almost every company's business.

The basic pre-condition is that messages to industry must be couched in clear language, but should be fully authoritative. It is also essential that the messages are taken to firms, rather than the Department offering national, London-based events. The programme delivery mechanism is becoming more locally-based, working through DTI Regional Offices, Training and Enterprise Councils, Business Link and so on.

The costs of the Managing in the 90s Programme are approximately £3 million per annum.

Skills and source material are identified through liaison with academic institutions and professional bodies. Indeed the majority of the material offered under the programme is developed in collaboration with non-governmental experts in such bodies.

The target market for the programme is chief executives and senior managers in businesses in all sectors and all regions of the U.K. These are identified through databases (specific and general) and other information available from numerous sources on an ad hoc basis.

Potential obstacles, risks etc. largely concern the ability to attract the right audience to events. These can be overcome by offering an attractive programme and targeting the market accurately.

It is difficult to be specific about demonstrable progress. Much depends on how this is defined. If it is defined in terms of broader recognition in the target market of the need to take action and then an indication that action has been taken, timescales can vary between eight years and three years. But the target market is continually changing and thus the programme needs to be a rolling one.

Typical steps include:

i) Establishing an outline plan for the programme;

ii) Developing contacts with providers of material, including academic institutions;

iii) Arranging for literature to be written and published;

iv) Arranging for seminar events to be organised;

v) Continual review of activities;

Steps (ii) to (iv) above take between 12 and 15 months.

4.5 Developing partnerships with industry

This entry takes the Department of Trade and Industry (DTI) as an example and concentrates on its "Managing in the 90s" programme and the sector Divisions of the Department. Moreover, successive governments have placed differing levels of emphasis on links with industry and this paper will largely reflect the current approach.

First, a number of the main industrial sectors are represented by sectoral Divisions of the Department of Trade and Industry. Each of these Divisions keeps in close contact with developments in its own industry or industries, gets to know its problems and successes and is able to act as a two-way link between the industries and Government. The sector Divisions are also in close touch with other parts of DTI and are therefore able to signpost firms correctly and also pass on a flow of up to date information wherever it is needed. The flow of information and assistance is far from being one-way. Government itself derives much valuable material from the contact. The bottom line is that best practice is best disseminated by business-to-business links. DTI facilitates this by featuring in much of its literature real experiences of companies.

DTI (and some other departments) have regional offices in major cities throughout the United Kingdom, whose task is to visit, inform and help local industry and groups of companies, exporters etc.

There is also an increasing emphasis on seconding industrialists to the public sector. This not only gives better and more up to date information to government departments but enables their advice to carry greater credibility with the target audience. Industry looks to DTI and other departments as a source of unbiased and impartial information, but it is important that it is closely related to the realities and demands of industry and commerce. DTI's primary role is as a catalyst.

The context for change

A strong, prosperous and competitive industry is clearly an advantage to any country and government has a role to play in supporting, encouraging and informing. The aim of U.K. Government policies is to achieve this and to equip U.K. industry by acting as a catalyst to improve the exchange of best practice, of innovative approaches and of ready access to government help and information, as described in the paragraphs above.

The policies of the U.K. Government in this field are aimed at:

- improving the competitiveness of U.K. business;
- informing, encouraging and standing alongside industry to help them face current challenges and problems;
- helping industries faced with the need for change to tackle it head on and develop a strategy;
- encouraging industries to share experience and best practice with their peers;
- producing authoritative information on current topics, e.g. the European Single Market;
- making advice and information available locally to industry via a network of sources, such as Training and Enterprise Councils (TECs) and One Stop Shops;
- encouraging innovation, in the widest sense, so that firms are able to progress dynamically.

Implementing change

There is also a number of initiatives aimed at meeting industry's needs. Currently, one emphasis is on the "Managing in the 90s" programme. Its purpose is to help companies address the challenges of world-wide economic uncertainty, changing markets, demographic change, saturation of demand, environmental concerns, increased competition from newcomers to the marketplace and a more discerning end-user.

A recent emphasis has been on innovation. This is not simply generating new products but far more an openness to and enthusiasm for ideas and developments of all types that will improve the performance and competitiveness of industry. The most successful companies in world industry innovate in this sense on a very large scale and many believe that this is the secret of their success.

The programme initially focused on four areas of industrial performance – design, production, purchasing and quality – and has recently been extended and updated to include marketing and new product introduction. It aims to cover further topics in the future.

"Managing into the 90s" aims to help companies adapt and change – not by telling them what to do so much as by spreading the message of encouragement and best practice. Much of this is achieved through high quality, informative publications and seminars (attended by more than 50,000). The aim is to inform and enthuse businesses so that they become better aware of best practice and in this way become better able to share it with others.

One of DTI's most successful schemes is called "Inside U.K. Enterprise". This scheme enables representatives of U.K. businesses to visit leading companies employing management practice in a wide range of product areas. Key personnel can see successful methods and ideas in practice and are able to speak directly to those able to pass on their knowledge and expertise. It is a concept which is now being adopted in several other countries.

Costs naturally depend on the extent of the action taken. Extensive and longstanding arrangements for partnership and contact with industry will naturally be costly in terms of staff time and promotional material and seminars of all types. However the expectation is that this expenditure is more than repaid by the economic benefits in the long-term.

Key stakeholders include the relevant Divisions of government and also staff at a senior, decision-taking level in industry and the relevant associations.

Programmes of any size are likely to take several years to bear any fruit. In the U.K., DTI launched the Enterprise Initiative, an overall banner under which much of the current material appears, in 1988. Similarly, the programme of "Managing in the 90s" has taken many months planning and introduction and is still very much an ongoing initiative.

4.6 A particular initiative in local empowerment: Inner City Task Forces

The Task Force Programme was one of the first to specify within its objectives the aim of promoting improved co-ordination at the local level between the activities of Central Government departments, local authorities and other organisations. This activity is equivalent to the building of local partnerships.

Task Forces have demonstrated the need for improved co-ordination and partnership in inner city policy at the local level and have also shown that it could be improved to the benefit of inner city residents.

The context for change

The Task Force Initiative was established because the inhabitants of inner city areas were, to a significant extent, unable to participate, or were prevented from participating effectively, in a modern, developed, free market economy. Thus they were not benefiting fully from the improvement in the performance of the economy which had occurred, and they continued to experience very high levels of unemployment. Moreover, existing national and regional government programmes were not sufficiently fine-tuned to help people in the inner city areas overcome their economic, social and environment disadvantages.

The Initiative is experimental in nature, pioneering new approaches to inner city problems which have been broadly identified as those of employment, enterprise, employability and, more recently, education. The rationale for the Initiative is the belief that government intervention is required to correct the failure of the market economy to benefit this portion of the population and the consequent necessity to provide a focal point for encouraging change within government, introducing greater sensitivity to the practical issues in areas of particular social and economic difficulty. The Initiative's aim is to improve targeting and enhance the benefit to local people of money channelled through existing central programmes. It also has its own budget to allocate to suitable projects in the areas in which it operates and encourages the participation of the private sector. The successful approaches which develop from this process will be adopted or encouraged more widely in urban policy.

Implementing change

The Inner City Task Forces are small teams which operate in sixteen of the most deprived urban areas. They come from a wide variety of backgrounds – central and local government, the private and voluntary sectors – and have a wide range of experience. They concentrate on the economic regeneration of designated inner city areas by improving local people's employment prospects, stimulating enterprise development and strengthening the capacity of communities to meet local needs.

Task Forces:

- work strategically to identify local problems and opportunities;
- determine their intentions and priorities (including an agreed exit strategy) through annual Action Plans;
- are temporary in nature, so they work with other key actors and organisations to improve the capacity of the local community to sustain the regeneration of the area after the Task Force leaves;
- support projects which promote the creation and safeguarding of jobs, the provision of education and training programmes, and the direct support of businesses;
- stimulate economic activity in the area by pump-priming private sector involvement and investment;
- target the needs of specific disadvantaged groups, especially ethnic minorities;
- develop community services, improve the environment, and reduce crime by supporting initiatives which provide training or jobs;
- develop innovatory approaches which are capable of wider application.

The successful features of the Inner Cities programme, identified in this paper, have been replicated/reflected in other mainstream programmes. For example, the notions of targeting, broking partnerships, involving local communities and capacity building, underpin later initiatives such as City Challenge. The current Task Forces have an economic remit. If required, this could be adapted to include a social or an environmental dimension. They can be managed centrally, regionally or by a local authority. They can be set up in towns as well as in large cities. In short, the Task Force model is capable of wide application.

U.K. experience suggests that the system needs to be simple, along the lines of the following:

- small teams of five or six committed and enthusiastic people;
- teams should work in tightly defined areas, with a specific remit to get certain things done;
- teams should be allowed a considerable degree of autonomy and flexibility in the way they carry out their tasks;
- programme managers need to develop a sophisticated system for monitoring performance, evaluating effectiveness and disseminating good practice.

The costs of the U.K.'s Inner Cities Task Force Initiative are approximately £22 million per annum, which accounts for only about two per cent of total government policy expenditure devoted specifically to the regeneration of inner cities. The average Task Force expenditure per project across the whole programme is less than £30,000. The "outside" contributions from government and private sector organisations are important. For every £1 spent of the Task Forces' own funds, about £1.60 was spent from the funds of partner organisations: 40p from the private sector (in cash or kind), £1.10 from elsewhere in the public sector and 10p from the voluntary sector. Each Task Force has a leader and staff of typically four or five and spends on average £11.4 million pounds per year of its own funds.

Skills include the ability to see through an innovative programme in an environment which may be difficult and challenging. Strong management, representational and diplomatic skills will be needed.

Key stakeholders include the local Task Force manager (choosing the right person is absolutely critical) and senior local authority officials. Clearly there will be other important local players in industry, voluntary groups and so on.

It is also important to monitor the effectiveness of the Task Forces. In the U.K.'s Inner City Task Forces, effectiveness is monitored internally, and evaluated externally, so that lessons learnt can be applied not only to other Task Forces, but also to mainstream government programmes.

The programme has been in existence for seven years and has had time to develop a successful track record. In some task force areas, clear, demonstrable results were being achieved within one or two years of their establishment.

4.7 Decentralisation

Decentralisation suggests removing from central government those functions which are no longer considered appropriate to it. It may also involve dispersing functions away from the traditional seat of government. Traditionally, much of the U.K. Government machine has been centred in London (Whitehall) and only relatively recently have significant "central" functions been moved to the provinces.

Moving functions away from government altogether may involve stopping the activities completely, contracting them out or privatising them. These aspects are addressed elsewhere in this publication, in particular in the entry on Market-Testing and Contracting Out of Services. Functions may also be entrusted to Agencies, a topic covered in the entry on Improving Productivity.

This entry therefore concentrates on the other aspect: relocation.

The context for change

Relocation is seen as a means of improving value for money and reducing costs, by reducing accommodation and staff costs and improving staff recruitment and retention. Locations away from the seat of government are likely to offer poorer employment prospects (at least this has been the case in the United Kingdom). As a result, moves to provincial locations have enabled the Government to recruit better quality staff at lower salaries. This has often proved to give greater savings than merely the reduced cost of accommodation.

Implementing change

U.K. Government departments are expected regularly to consider relocation to sites offering best value for money, easier labour markets and increased operational efficiency.

Originally, there was a centrally-directed dispersal programme, under which a number of departments decided to move staff away from London. However, the current focus is on a delegated, value-for-money approach introduced in 1987. This places responsibility for taking relocation decisions with departmental Ministers who are best placed to take into account all the various factors. There is therefore no longer a centrally-directed programme, but the Treasury acts as a central source of experience and expertise. Departments report each year to the Treasury on their progress with, and plans for, relocation.

Discontinuation, privatisation and contracting out of an activity should be considered before relocation. If none of these options is practical, relocation is a further possibility.

The relocation review programme for most departments is likely to include four main stages:

i) A preliminary review to identify the main blocks of work which, on the face of it, are the most suitable candidates for relocation. However, it is best to look at every part of the department, without exception, because otherwise some areas will claim that they ought to be exempt from scrutiny (when in fact they are merely trying to defend the status quo).

ii) Consultation with the key stakeholding departments (those responsible for regional policy and local industries/employment), territorial departments and any department responsible for administering government-owned buildings and property.

iii) Preparation of a detailed study of alternative locations, their costs and benefits. At the end of this stage, decisions in principle to relocate may be made by departmental Ministers.

iv) Appraisal of alternative property options within the chosen area for relocation.

If going ahead with a move, it is best to have a dedicated relocation project team. They will work with management to maintain good communications with the staff involved. Identifying possible obstacles is achieved through consulting the main stakeholders and through awareness of the practical lessons on the appraisal and project management of recent relocations shared by other relocating departments. Those who have moved offices successfully are likely to be enthusiasts for the methods used and will probably have identified even better ones in some areas.

This naturally depends on the size of the project. If a thorough review of locations is to take place, involving proper cost/benefit analysis, it will certainly take two or three months for even a medium-sized block of work (perhaps 100 staff). This provides only the information on which to take a decision. The actual decision to relocate will involve much more: convincing senior management and Ministers, overcoming possible opposition from staff and making detailed plans to move the work. Experience shows that all this cannot be achieved in less than one to two years.

SECTION 5: MAKING MANAGEMENT MORE EFFECTIVE

5.1 A particular initiative in enhancing management skills: The Department of Trade and Industry

5.2 Improving management information systems

5.3 Improving information technology support

5.4 Management development

5.5 Improving internal management advisory capacity

5.6 Improving the management of external consultants

5.1 A particular initiative in enhancing management skills: The Department of Trade and Industry

The 1988 White Paper entitled "Improving Management in Government: The Next Steps" recommended that all departments should undertake a review of training and development.

This entry focuses on the developments which flowed from that in one U.K. Ministry, the Department of Trade and Industry (DTI). An outside consultancy which specialised in industrial training carried out the review in DTI and recommended that training and development should be competence-based.

The context for change

In 1991 the Permanent Secretary launched the Managing and Developing People Initiative. This emphasised that the main responsibility for development lay with the individual, helped and encouraged by line management. The changes were designed to bring about an improvement in management skills across the Department, together with a recognition that, to manage better, good management needs to be given higher priority.

Essentially, the Department has concentrated on two main strands of policy in enhancing management skills:

- introducing competence-based personal development schemes; and
- improving management training.

Both of these areas are inter-related and are equally important. The moves towards the use of the competence approach to personal development and the greater delegation to line management or functions formerly carried out at the centre are mirrored in other departments and are in line with best practice in the private sector.

Implementing change

The DTI has introduced competence-based development schemes for staff at AA/AO, EO-G7 (including Scientific and Technical grades), Secretarial/Typing grades and G5/6. (AA and AO are clerical grades, EO-G7 represent junior/middle/senior management grades and G5/6 cover senior managers, though not the most senior.)

The development schemes are aimed at helping staff to identify their work-related skills needs and, with line management help, to identify the most effective ways of meeting them. There are also proposals, being pursued by the Office of Public Service and Science, to extend the competence approach to the Senior Open Structure (the most senior grades). Departmental training provision has been tailored to reflect these competence frameworks. A job advertising scheme, covering EO, HEO and SEO vacancies has also been introduced. This places the responsibility on line management for recruitment and selection of staff and emphasises the importance of good interviewing and decision-making skills. Responsibility for decisions on probation, poor performance and inefficiency, formerly held within the central personnel function, has been delegated to line managers.

Until 1991, the DTI's training budget was held centrally and the in-house training provider offered a range of personal development and management courses. These courses were listed in the Department's training prospectus and staff were encouraged to apply for those that they felt would best meet their training needs. The Staff Appraisal system helped with the process of identifying needs, as it focused the line manager's mind on staff development.

Since 1991, budgets for training have been devolved to individual management units. Personnel Training Services (PTS), as the in-house training provider, have designed and tailored events to complement the competence-based schemes now operating in the Department. In addition to those trainer led courses, PTS also provide:

- a training and management consultancy service;
- an open learning unit, which provides a range of technology-based training aids, including computer-based training.

DTI managers are, of course free to spend their budgets with other training providers, for example the Civil Service College and many independent firms and colleges who offer specialised training in particular areas.

The changes taking place in the DTI that have implications for management training include:

- market-testing;
- the Citizen's Charter and the increased importance of providing a quality service;
- the restructuring of HQ Divisions, as a result of recent changes in

government policy.

The basic requirements for success are:

- a demonstrable commitment from the top levels of management;
- a willingness on the part of senior/middle management to manage and implement change;
- training, organisational and individual learning needs to be correctly identified, with management units developing training strategies, setting out their training priorities, the options available for meeting them and the roles and responsibilities of the staff concerned.

Identifying the necessary skills hinges crucially on consultation and discussion about people's actual job-related requirements. This is now increasingly the subject of dialogue between job-holder and line manager, with the initiative coming from the former.

The key stakeholders will normally be identified as those charged with managing the change and those affected by it.

The potential obstacles and risks to success stem from resistance to change, and from the difficulties of planning medium to long-term in an unsettled and uncertain environment. It is generally agreed that change of the kind represented by these types of initiative can take upwards of five years, given favourable conditions, to become embedded in the culture of the organisation. Management units are encouraged to evaluate training so that they can prove that the money and time invested has been instrumental in improving performance.

Typical steps or stages in implementing a competence-based system are:

- identify the need for change;
- field research and consultation to highlight the nature of the desired outcome;
- draw up draft material;
- pilot this material with selected staff;
- further consultation/validation;
- introduce material/scheme/initiative;

- monitor effectiveness;
- review.

In all management development training, the following steps are vital:

- identify the learning needs for the specific target group;
- decide upon the most effective method of meeting the needs, e.g. work-based training, formal training course, open learning etc.;
- carry out the training;
- evaluate the effectiveness of the training.

5.2 Improving management information systems

Information systems are the information technology paper-based systems which support business needs.

Government departments have established information systems in the principal areas of their business, for example:

- personnel records;
- finance;
- physical resources (including accommodation);
- procurement (purchasing).

The context for change

Information is a vital resource, and requires careful planning to ensure it is best applied to meet business aims and objectives. This makes it the concern of senior management. The use of information technology (IT) in almost all areas of government business means that adequate support must be in place to ensure smooth, continuous development and/or operations of the various systems.

A fundamental question that concerns the introduction of any new system, or the upgrading of an existing one, is whether it should be paper-based or computer-based. Available finance, the number of people who need to have access to the new or improved system, and the need for easy interrogation are important factors when making a decision.

Various management information systems must be able to interface with one another, i.e. the information they contain brought together and produced on a common basis. This need for information to be used flexibly, with other in-house or out-house systems, is a major consideration when considering introducing or upgrading an IT-based information system.

Implementing change

U.K. experience indicates that a strategic approach benefits the customer in terms of identifying and prioritising requirements for information systems, and ensuring compatibility with other existing and planned systems. It also benefits the approving authority (whether elsewhere within the organisation, or, for larger expenditure, the Treasury) in providing a backcloth against which to consider each proposal for expenditure.

The alternative of ad hoc acquisition of individual machines and systems leaves management with less flexibility to change working practices, and thereby reduces the overall return on investment in information systems and IT.

Strategic planning for information systems is concerned with:

- understanding the aims and objectives of the business;

- establishing the information requirements of the business;

- outlining the systems to provide the information;

- determining the role of technology in supporting the information systems;

- agreeing policies and plans to develop and implement the information systems;

- determining the role and use of resources to achieve the information systems required;

- managing, reviewing and evolving the strategy.

Departments have long recognised the importance of managment information systems and, drawing on both private and public sector experience, have developed systems to meet their own specific needs. The Government believes that such systems are not being used to their full advantage and the Efficiency Unit is conducting a scrutiny to determine departmental and Agency needs, to consider best practice in both the public and private sectors and to make recommendations for future development. The results of the scrutiny should assist managers in the efficient and effective allocation of resources and in planning to achieve the required efficiency savings.

A particular initiative in improving management information systems: The Department of Trade and Industry

Amongst the principal DTI systems are:

- FINMIS (Financial Management Information System)
- PERMIS (Personnel Management Information System)
- PREMIS (Physical Resources Management Information System)

- SAMIS (Selective Assistance Management Information System)
- FINMIS (Financial Management Information System)

FINMIS (Financial Management Information System)

Functions

The principal objective of FINMIS is to provide an integrated accounting, budgeting and financial reporting system.

FINMIS:

- provides senior departmental management and "cost centre" managers with comprehensive financial information on both a regular and an ad hoc basis;

- maintains details of running costs and capital income of the Department by "cost type" within cost centre, and also provides budgeting, forecasting and estimating facilities;

- receives data through interfaces with various other systems (e.g. RESULTS, PERMIS, HM TREASURY PAYROLL, PREMIS AND RECHARGING STATIONERY, TYPING, REPROGRAPHICS, COMPUTER SERVICES).

Data can be input through on-line terminals.

System profile

This is a very high-profile system which is used by up to 150 senior and cost centre managers within the Department. The system is essential for the efficient monitoring and control of the Department's costs and 'Programme Spend'.

In addition, some 2,000 users have potential access to the system.

PERMIS (Personnel Management Information System)

Functions

PERMIS's requirement is to provide assistance in the management of the Department's personnel records.

PERMIS:

- provides a central register of all permanent staff currently working in the Department, and those who have left since 1 April 1985 (it does not include Ministers and consultants);
- records information about staff's academic qualifications, skills, job history, staff reports, seniority, age, grade etc.;
- caters for the provision of manpower statistics and forecasting;
- maintains promotion boarding and training records and an accurate record of staff cost centres, via the Date Input Routes (DIR) module;
- interfaces with various other systems (including FINMIS and PREMIS);
- must be able to supply additional facilities as users identify needs.

System profile

This is a high-profile system which is used by about 400 Personnel Management users and about 240 DIR users. The majority of users consider the system essential for them to carry out their duties.

PREMIS(Physical ResourcesManagement Information System)

Functions

PREMIS helps the Department manage its physical resources.

PREMIS:

- provides senior Departmental management, cost centre managers and other line managers with comprehensive information, allowing them to manage the utilisation of accommodation, space and equipment resources within the Department;
- provides local accommodation staff and other system-users with an effective tool to assist them with the efficient performance of their duties;
- maintains details of premises, rooms, occupancy and telephone numbers, together with the relevant cost centre details;

- interfaces with various other systems (e.g. FINMIS, PREMIS);
- must be able to supply additional facilities as users identify needs.

System profile

This is a high-profile system which is used by about 90 Accommodation officers and managers and about 240 DIR users. The majority of users consider the system essential for them to carry out their duties.

SAMIS (Selective Assistance Management Information System)

Functions

SAMIS's principal objective is to provide a system for collecting, aggregating and analysing all information required for the sponsorship of U.K. industry by the Department. It is a computerised case recording system which is used more for management information purposes than for case administration.

SAMIS:

- records key information for cases under a variety of different assistance schemes, and information on manufacturing units in the U.K. employing ten or more people;
- provides an integrated system holding the information needed to control all financial assistance schemes and projects for industry administered by the DTI (and now expanded to include Consultancy Assistance from the DTI's Enterprise Initiative Scheme);
- provides management information for:
    - the administration of individual schemes;
    - forecasting future resource requirements and case loads for future operations;
    - briefing Ministers and senior officials;
    - preparing answers to Parliamentary Questions (PQs);
    - evaluating the effectiveness of the schemes in operation.

- specifically holds information for the following functions:
  - Records of Serious Enquiries: details of companies which have expressed an interest which is expected to materialise into a full application;
  - Records of Application: details of all full applications made;
  - Records of Application Results: details of the result of an application once a decision has been reached;
  - Records of Claims: details of claims received and forecasted payments;
  - Records of Payments: details of payments made;
  - Changes to Company/Project Details: company or project details where necessary.
- receives and passes data through interfaces with other systems.

System Profile

This is a comparatively low-profile system which does not run to any tight schedule. It has an estimated 200 users within the Department. The Department has been actively assessing the feasibility of a replacement for SAMIS.

5.3 Improving information technology support

Information technology (IT) is a term commonly used to encompass the methods and techniques used in information handling and retrieval by automatic means, including computing, telecommunications and office systems. Information systems (IS) are the IT and non-IT based systems which support business needs.

IT support can be defined in two ways:

- the support which IT can provide to information systems; or
- the support which is needed for IT-based systems which have been, or are to be introduced.

In terms of the second, narrower definition, IT support can take a number of forms: from the strategic (the assessment of a system's needs and the subsequent system-development and implementation) to the entirely practical (e.g. maintenance of a local computer network or individual machines).

The context for change

Central government in the U.K. invests more than £2 billion a year in information systems (IS) and employs 20,000 staff to install and operate the information and telecommunications systems that support internal administration and help to deliver services to the public. Before very long, virtually every civil servant will have some access to information technology.

As government's needs for IS become more demanding and complex, the IT industry's range of products and services is also increasing. The increasing use of IT equipment in all areas of business activity has brought the need for adequate support to be in place to ensure smooth, continuous development and/or operation of any system.

Implementing change

CCTA: The Government Centre for Information Systems

Within the U.K. Civil Service, a body called CCTA, the Government Centre for Information Systems (part of the Office of Public Service and Science, itself part of the Cabinet Office) is responsible for promoting business effectiveness and efficiency in government through the use of information systems. While CCTA's customers are government departments and executive agencies, HM Treasury Expenditure Divisions, and certain public bodies sponsored by Departments, its business environment is wider, and includes European and other national governments, European Community institutions, international standards bodies, the academic world and the IS supply and service industry. It provides specific services to government departments and agencies, helps them plan their spending on information systems, and advises them on the best use of their information technology, e.g. through help in evaluating the various systems available, against needs and value for money. It both publishes advice and guidance on best practice throughout IS/IT and makes available direct support to individual customers, where such services add greater value for money or where the private sector is unable or unwilling to meet the service requirement. CCTA encourages customers to take a forward-looking strategic approach to the use of IS/IT, in relation to those systems which underpin business activity and support management. CCTA does not differentiate between these two systems, but promotes incorporation of both into an effective IT strategy from which plans for individual systems and projects may be produced.

CCTA is keen to see business managers, rather than technologists, set the future direction for the use of IS in support of business objectives. Increasingly, business managers are seen as "owning" IS, whereas formerly technologists owned IT.

Management information systems (MIS) are just one of many applications that underpin the business of government. Therefore, CCTA does not seek to develop expertise on individual types of system. Some MIS needs are shared by all organisations; others are unique and require bespoke software. Either way, the costs can be considerable; and there is sometimes a tendency for management to attach a lower priority to MIS than other business applications.

The technological complexity of IT equipment and systems, in comparison with paper-based information systems, means that specialist knowledge must be available, either in-house or through private firms providing services on the basis of a business contract (or, sometimes, on a combined basis, i.e. an in-house team working between system-users and the outside contractors).

IT support will not come necessarily from equipment or systems specialists alone. It is, after all, business managers who are instrumental in determining the reasons behind any strategy and, by implication, what a system should be capable of producing. In general terms, the technology which is introduced should be subservient to system needs. So, any group of persons, which acts in an advisory or support capacity, may well be formed of strategists (perhaps senior management), system users, and customers (where different from system users), as well as IT specialists.

The need for a strategic approach to the development of new IS/IT systems is discussed in the paper on management information systems. Most departments will have several of these; they may, for example, cover such areas as personnel records, finance, physical resources (including accommodation), and procurement (purchasing). Within a particular department, there is usually a need for the various management information systems to "interface" with one another. They may even need to interface with a system in another department.

Any government, which is considering introducing IT, and the necessary support should assess the need for its information to be used flexibly with other information systems, either in-house or out-house, and the extent to which information on different areas needs to be brought together and produced on a common basis.

Strategic planning for information systems is concerned with:

- understanding the aims and objectives of the business;
- establishing the information requirements of the business;
- outlining the systems to provide the information;
- determining the role of technology in supporting the information systems;
- agreeing policies and plans to develop and implement the information systems;
- determining the role and use of resources to achieve the information systems required;
- managing, reviewing and evolving the strategy.

Behind strategic planning is a series of fundamental questions:

- What is the scope?
- Where are we now?
- Where do we want to be?
- How do we get there?

The following stages are fundamental to the determination of IT support for IT-based activities, and its implementation at project level. They are adjusted according to local circumstances:

- Ensure that, in principle, the necessary *finance and staff resources* for any system, and support services, are in place or can be made available when needed (though more accurate figures may not be apparent until a later stage);

- Establish a *project board* comprised of persons who have the greatest interest in ensuring that any IT-based system(s) succeeds;

- Decide, through the project board, what the *objective* of the IT system is, i.e. what will be its uses and products, and whether it should be based on a "strategic" approach;

- Devise an *action plan* that encompasses what is to be achieved, at what time, and by whom (this stage will include decisions on whether IT can be sourced 'off the shelf', and the support service bought in, or whether IT will have to be specially developed and a wholly or partly in-house support team formed);

- Start *pre-implementation actions,* e.g. decisions on the need to issue tenders; devising any tender specifications; issuing tender documents or advertising their availability; evaluating bids, and choosing supplier(s); establishing contract(s);

- Put *implementation-review procedures* in place (these will have been foreseen in the action plan);

- Start *project implementation.*

Since no two government businesses are the same, there are no common answers to questions of costs and timescales etc. These vary considerably from department to department.

5.4 Management development

The context for change

It is now a well-established principle that individual departments and Executive Agencies are responsible for training and developing their own staff. The role of the Cabinet Office, Office of Public Service and Science (OPSS) is to encourage them to make progressive improvements in staff management, development and training in support of their own operational requirements or specific business needs. They do this by:

- identifying and promoting good practice;
- providing information and advice, either on a one-to-one basis or through a range of networks;
- developing training and other approaches in support of central initiatives;
- co-ordinating consortium projects to help departments and agencies tackle new issues, thus identifying good practice for wider dissemination; and
- running conferences and workshops on topical issues.

The main development programmes in operation throughout the Civil Service are:

- The Top Management Programme (TMP);
- Development of Senior Managers (DSM);
- The Senior Professional Administrative Training Scheme (SPATS);
- Management Development Programmes (MDP);
- The Fast Stream (AT/HEOD) Scheme.

Implementing change

OPSS have a general co-ordinating role in relation to these schemes and hold regular meetings with the relevant personnel/training managers from departments and agencies. Among topics studied on the MDP Co-ordinators' Group, for example, are:

- the use of computer-based needs analysis systems in MDPs;

- developing standards for competence frameworks;
- the use of assessment centres for the selection of participants; and
- how best to review MDPs.

The ***Top Management Programme*** is an intensive residential programme for senior managers run by the Cabinet Office (OPSS). Its participants come in equal numbers from the public and private sectors. Four programmes are run each year. Each lasts four weeks, followed by an additional two weeks, primarily for civil servants.

The objectives of the first four weeks focus on:

- understanding the changing context of management;
- understanding and working with others;
- formulating and implementing strategies to meet the challenge of change;
- improving performance;
- leading and motivating people.

The two additional weeks of the programme are to enable civil servants, or others who are interested, to apply the experience of the first four weeks specifically to work in government, and to improve certain essential skills.

There are two key themes: *change* and *top management*. Sessions on change aim to broaden understanding of changes in the environment (economic, social, international, political), which participants must know about to lead their organisations successfully. Sessions on top management examine key elements essential to good leadership, including strategic thinking and managing people and money effectively.

The participants are high fliers from the public and private sectors. Typically they:

- are aged 35-50 (though this is not a rigid rule);
- have significant further potential which could take them to the highest positions in their organisations;
- have a proven record of success and breadth of experience which the programme will complement and extend;
- are able to hold their own with other participants of high quality and diverse backgrounds.

Civil Servants reaching Grade 3 (Under Secretary) level are normally nominated by their departments.

From 1985 to 1991, there was a centrally driven programme for the development of senior managers (the Senior Management Development Programme - SMDP). In 1991, it was decided that departments and agencies should take more direct responsibility for making their own arrangements for senior management development in line with their business needs.

The aims of senior management development remain as before:

- better preparation for future top managers (i.e. those with potential to reach Grade 3);

- greater effectiveness in the Senior Management Grades (Grades 4-7) for all articipants, whether or not they are likely to reach more senior levels.

Departments' and Agencies' systems will continue to develop senior managers through integrated programmes involving a series of relevant jobs, formal and less structured methods of training and other methods such as projects, secondments and open and distance learning.

Progress relies on individual responsibility and self-help. Line managers have a supporting but important role in agreeing objectives, helping to meet them and ensuring that they fit in with the priorities and business needs of the department.

To assist with the identification of development needs, several departments and agencies are now working on development frameworks for senior managers at Grades 4-7. In the meantime, many departmental schemes still make use of the original SMDP competence framework.

The ***Senior Professional Administrative Training Scheme*** (SPATs) aims to give specialists with senior management potential the opportunity to broaden their experience of management reasonably early in their careers.

The scheme is open to staff at Grade 7 and equivalent levels and, exceptionally, to staff one grade above and one grade below, subject to their possessing the recognised potential to rise to at least Grade 5.

The scheme has two main elements: a three-week course at the Civil Service College and an administrative posting.

- *A three-week course at the Civil Service College*

  The course aims to equip specialists with the additional administrative skills needed in their experience postings (see below), and covers subjects such as constitutional law; the relationship between ministers and officials; drafting replies to parliamentary questions and briefing ministers for parliamentary debates and appearances before select committees.

  Before each course begins, the College contacts participants to identify their particular training needs (for example, some may wish to improve their written communication skills). Before attending the SPATS course, members are also asked to undertake in their own time a policy studies exercise, spread over several months and guided by tutors, in which they select, with departmental agreement, a particular policy decision and then examine how that decision was reached. This is designed to place course members in a better position to draw practical benefits from the course.

- *An administrative posting*

  The administrative posting of about two years is an integral part of the scheme, although a programme of short attachments and project work will also be acceptable where departments regard this as appropriate. The sole criterion is that the posting or postings should be of a quality and duration both to provide candidates with challenging work and to broaden their experience.

Management Development Programmes (MDPs) began to be set up in 1985 to ensure a steady supply of good quality staff to fill posts at Grade 7 through a more systematic approach to staff development at EO, HEO and SEO levels.

It is for each department to devise a development programme to meet its needs. For example, selection procedures vary between departments. There are, however, certain key components to each programme.

- *A planned postings policy*: this enables staff on a programme to obtain experience in a range of posts which make managerial and intellectual demands and develop the qualities required for the future. Postings are tailored carefully to the individual's needs and build up a balanced profile of experience.

- *Development within jobs:* whilst movement between jobs is important in cultivating flexibility and a range of experience, participants are constantly given the opportunity to show initiative, to make decisions and to take responsibility for human and financial resources.

- *Integrated training:* this need not be confined to formal training but may consist of other learning opportunities such as open learning and self-instruction. The Civil Service College publishes a guide to those training courses which are especially suitable for MDP participants.

- *Project work, special postings, secondments and short-term attachments* provide other development opportunities. Project work presents the challenge of managing a piece of work and pacing progress as well as demonstrating creative and intellectual flair. Special postings, secondments and short-term attachments, which need not involve a change of location, can offer exposure to unfamiliar environments and problems which may broaden the perspective of staff.

The AT/HEO(D) Scheme is designed for the intensive development of a small cadre of high quality staff who will, if they meet the demanding standard required, achieve early promotion to Grade 7.

A majority of ATs and HEO(D)s typically find themselves employed in the headquarters of departments, often working in policy divisions, although an increasing number are directly employed on operational delivery in Agencies. They move fairly quickly through a carefully selected pattern of demanding postings lasting about one year each, designed to give them a feel for the range of work carried out in their department and develop the talents and skills needed at senior levels. ATs and HEO(D)s are expected to make an effective contribution to the work of the department and show the potential which justifies early promotion. Some of the work, particularly that connected with Parliament, Ministers' private offices or senior officials, means regular long hours, often under pressure. Although training is mainly on the job, formal training is provided on a modular basis by the Civil Service College.

ATs and HEO(D)s are expected to be able to:

- deal effectively with people at all levels (including staff);
- defend a case lucidly and persuasively;
- make sound judgements;
- accept responsibility;
- manage resources efficiently (both financial and human);
- work hard and quickly.

Entrants to the Fast Stream under the age of 26 are graded AT until they reach the age of 26 or have served two years in the grade, after which they become HEO(D).

Entrants over the age of 26 and HEOs are graded HEO(D) from the outset.

The two methods of entry are:

i) As an internal candidate, for serving staff who are in a grade below SEO level; and whose department can provide an annual report or good equivalent; and who are nominated by their department.

This method of entry is not confined to graduates, and Civil Service departments encourage suitable candidates from any background to come forward.

ii) As an external candidate, for graduates who have a degree with at least second class honours. Serving EOs and HEOs may be exempt from this provision if they have passed probation. External candidates are required to sit a qualifying test.

Successful internal and external candidates are invited to the Civil Service Selection Board (CSSB), which comprises two days of written and group exercises, tests and interview.

Following CSSB, all candidates who are considered to have a chance of being successful are interviewed by the Final Selection Board, which is chaired by the First Civil Service Commissioner or her deputy, sitting with two civil servants and two outside members.

A review of Fast Stream recruitment has recently been completed and the Government is considering the recommendations.

The Civil Service College exists to provide a centre of excellence for developing managerial and professional skills amongst civil servants, and promoting best practice throughout government, both in management and key professional areas. It operates as an Agency and provides:

- management training for both civil servants and the private sector at, or aspiring to, relatively senior positions;

- specialist training in key areas or at advanced levels;

- related consultancy and research.

It aims to:

- reflect in its work the particular needs of government;

- support the initiatives and policies of government, in particular those affecting the management of the Civil Service in departments and Agencies within government;

- develop professionalism and to provide training leading to externally validated qualifications.

The College's close understanding of the working context and problems of its customers in government give it a unique position. In teaching the best of today's management approaches and skills, as tasks and disciplines of government become more business-like, the College can offer unrivalled practicality and relevance to their needs. Most courses are short and intensive: the average length is under four days. They offer the opportunity to work with counterparts from elsewhere in the Civil Service and provide a forum for the interchange of ideas and best practices.

The primary task is to identify clearly areas and groups where management potential exists and to have a system for harnessing it effectively. It is important to note that managers are not drawn exclusively from generalist or administrative fields, hence the importance of the SPATS scheme in the U.K. which is aimed at Scientific and Professional grade staff.

The costs of investing in people are significant. The scale can be illustrated by considering AT/HEO(D) training in the U.K. Although training is mainly on the job, there is a target of 20 days of formal training per year in the first two years of service, diminishing in subsequent years to give an overall average of 15 days per year. This is a substantial commitment in terms of staff costs, given that officers are unable during the training period to fulfil their normal duties. The investment is repaid in future potential.

Supporting material

Management and Development Programmes in the Civil Service, ISBN 0-7115-0156-4 1988

5.5 Improving internal management advisory capacity

In the U.K., departments have flexibility to adopt their own management advisory systems, provided that they ensure value for money by controlling the use of resources. There are inter-departmental links to encourage the sharing of good practice in which the Treasury exercises a central role.

All major departments have access to internal expertise to provide assurance about the use of resources, especially staff. These are normally known as Staff Inspection or Manpower Audit teams. Most departments also have in-house management consultancies, upon whose services line managers can draw (sometimes on a repayment basis, in competition with outside suppliers). In some departments, Ministers have decided to abolish the internal advisory function and to buy all such services from external suppliers, and in others the function has been market-tested.

There is increasing movement among internal advisory teams towards accreditation under BS 5750/ISO 9000, together with an emphasis on quality systems and customer service.

There has been extended debate about whether advice to management should be imposed by the department centrally or whether managers should be free to select services on a consultancy basis. Several departments have decided to split the two functions to avoid conflict of interests.

Training standards for Staff Inspection teams are set by the Treasury, in consultation with departments. Staff on these teams are trained centrally, with a view to applying consistent standards across the Civil Service.

The context for change

There are links with quality management, market-testing, continued ministerial pressure to reduce staff numbers, and continued and growing pressures to reduce overall expenditure. The Citizen's Charter is encouraging departments to ensure that their systems are adequate.

Consistent with government policies for optimal devolution and delegation, responsibility for these services lies with departments, not the centre. However, the centre has a role to bring some elements together and to undertake such aspects as standard setting, which individual departments could not themselves do. There is growing awareness at the centre of departments that delegation must be accompanied by carefully determined control and assurance mechanisms.

The policies on exposing services to competition (especially market-testing) have increased awareness of the need to be efficient and to meet management requirements.

Implementing change

This depends on whether an organisation is setting up internal management advice services where none previously existed or whether the aim is to improve the services that are currently available. In both cases clear roles and responsibilities need to be established, in particular whether the service is to be imposed or offered on a consultancy basis (or perhaps a combination of the two). In general, U.K. experience indicates that the two need to be kept quite separate if conflicts of interest are to be avoided and managers are free to use the consultancy role to the full, without fear of imposed solutions or recriminations.

Staff need to be chosen carefully. A certain type of officer is best for assignment and consultancy work: one with tact and presentational skills, willingness to challenge the status quo, vision to see how things can be improved, ability to express themselves clearly, both orally and on paper. Essentially, these are practical people, not those with their heads in policy clouds.

Costs should not be an issue. Good advice teams will make proposals that will save their costs many times over. Extensive use of external consultants may be expensive, especially if they are not familiar with the public service environment. Market-testing can also be expensive in management and staff time and quality system accreditation costs are likely to be up to £20,000 per department.

Stakeholders are senior managers (those who should use the services), managers of in-house consultancies (those who deliver) and any central authority, such as the Treasury in the U.K., who have an interest in value for money and overall departmental systems.

Six months to a year should see good progress in improving standards, but it is an ongoing process and the optimal point is always just out of reach.

Improving any advisory system involves project management with a "Management of Change" flavour. It will involve identifying where the organisation wants to go, identifying the stakeholders, establishing action plans and monitoring progress. It is important in the consultancy field to carry out research among customers to judge their perception of the service provided. Regular customer satisfaction questionnaires and appropriate corrective action where necessary are vital factors in improving performance.

5.6 Improving the management of external consultants

U.K. Government departments use consultants from the private sector and from academic institutions in a variety of ways. They provide expert advice, either in disciplines or from a full and comprehensive understanding of how a specialist area operates. The decision to engage the services of consultants is therefore usually taken because in-house resources either are not available when needed or do not yet exist. Ideally, the use of consultants should mean a transfer of expertise to in-house resources.

It is important to follow the right procedures when commissioning consultants – to secure value for money, to avoid exposing departments to unforeseen contractual commitments and to set up a visible, auditable trail of public sector expenditure.

Divisions which wish to engage external consultants should bear in mind that a considerable amount of management time must be set aside from the decision to undertake the project to the receipt of the final report. It is also important to remember that consultants should not be taken on to fill permanent staff posts. No consultancy team, irrespective of size, and no individual consultant will work full-time on your project. They will spend some days each week, the number fluctuating according to the stage reached in the life of the project. Consultants should not be regarded as employees and salaried. Their fees and the reimbursement of expenses should be paid for out of programme spend, not running costs.

Individual departments have a small group of staff carrying out tendering and contractual procedures and guidance is available centrally from HM Treasury's Accountancy Policy Division. HM Treasury issue to all departments and agencies an index of management consultants who are willing to work in the public sector. Most individual departments supplement this with their own databases of potential consultants.

The context for change

The primary objective of departmental policy on tendering and contracting must be to ensure value for money. Funds have been voted by Parliament, to whom the department is accountable.

Best practice is generally set out by HM Treasury and much of it is contained in their booklet entitled "Seeking Help from Management Consultants", addressed to line managers in government departments. Individual departments also set out guidance to line managers.

In other respects, best practice has evolved with experience, as tendering units have developed improvements to the system. In general, these are embodied in local rules and procedures and are set out in revisions to the notices to line managers.

Several consistent dimensions have emerged in the U.K. regarding best practice:

- There must be propriety in tendering matters, to make competitive tendering the standard and single tender action the exception. There may of course be low-value contracts where competitive tendering is not cost-effective, either for the department or the consultants themselves.

- Strenuous efforts are needed to ensure freedom from bias and collusion. A central, stand-alone unit handling the tendering procedures can ensure that all tenders received are properly recorded and held securely. It is regarded as unsatisfactory for the commissioning division to be involved in this procedure.

- It is important that procedures are clearly documented, as is the action taken by individual officers of the department. The reasons for decisions being taken and courses of action adopted must be clearly recorded and must be auditable.

- In order to avoid complacency, cosiness and lack of competition creeping in, it is wise to spread the base of those invited to bid. This is achieved by competitive bidding. The introduction of new consultants to the bidding process can produce unexpected winners who introduce fresh, new, creative thinking on possible solutions to problems.

Most departments use selection meetings. These are useful because they involve meeting the people who will do the job, providing an opportunity to question the consultancy team who will actually be delivering the written word; to question and probe on past similar experience; and to explore the proposed allocation of human and financial resources through the life of the project. It also gives the opportunity to indicate that proposed fees may be too high and perhaps that the very good, rather than the exceptionally thorough, is actually what is wanted.

The procedures for engaging external consultants are closely linked to procedures on purchasing goods, works and other services. There are also links with market-testing and contracting out; and with meeting the demands of the EC Directives on goods, works and services (which require that many large public contracts are made available for tendering by firms from all member states).

Implementing change

In the U.K., the following are prerequisites for establishing/improving mechanisms for managing external consultants:

- selection of responsible officials, skilled in negotiation with consultants and judgement of their proposals;

- carefully worked out procedures to ensure consistency and fairness of treatment and avoidance of errors;

- carefully maintained record of correspondence with consultants.

Commissioning/Client Divisions are required to address the following questions:

- Have they set aside enough management time?

- Are they able to manage and criticise constructively?

- Will they check that invoices represent fully the services delivered, according to the terms of the signed contract?

- Are they available to answer consultants' queries fully?

- Is there clear understanding as to where the project fits into the overall work of the Division?

- How are the results of what the consultants have done measured? Project managers should be asked to feed back their experience and record any resulting savings etc.

Tendering/contracting units are required to:

- understand the commissioning Division's needs, so that they are fully covered in the contract;

- be flexible in applying the tendering and contracting rules (i.e. they can be bent on the odd occasion, but never broken!);

- understand the intention behind each of the clauses in the contract, to be able to answer questions from the commissioning Division and the consultants;

- develop a good working relationship with the departmental lawyers, so that there is quick access if difficult problems arise.

The main potential risks are:

with Line Managers:

- over-emphasising independence and authority, at the experience of a reasonable level of central control.

with Consultants:

- taking the Client Division for granted;
- second-guessing and getting it wrong;
- incurring expenditure over and above the level in the signed contract;
- doing extra work without having got agreement in advance, but still expecting the Division to pay;
- changing the team members during the life of the project without informing the client;
- failing to keep to deadlines;
- late delivery of the report;
- poor written work;
- failure to follow up and build on the success of one contract.

Some of the typical stages in improving the management of external consultants include the following:

- Identify what is lacking in the existing programme. Should external consultants prepare a report?
- Use a customer survey to judge the effectiveness of the existing programme;
- Ask a selection of consultants how the department can improve its act;
- Consider what consultancy skills the department will need in the future;

- Careful consideration of the aims and objectives of the proposed improved programme;
- Check whether the standard contract clauses are still legally correct? Can they be put in plainer language?
- Are there any acts or laws now in force that bear on regularly used contract clauses, which therefore require amendment?
- Does the organisation use standard forms which could do with modernisation?
- What process, if any, exists to vet new consultants?
- Should the existing list of consultants be weeded out?

Supporting material

HM Treasury's booklet "Seeking Help from Management Consultants", HMSO, ISBN 0 11 560030-2, 1990, 2.50

SECTION 6: IMPROVING THE MANAGEMENT OF FINANCE

6.1 Internal audit

6.2 External auditing

6.3 Accruals-based accounting, assessing value for money, and introducing capital charging

6.4 Estate management

6.5 Improving procurement and purchasing procedures

6.6 End year flexibility

6.1 Internal audit

Internal audit is responsible for the systematic and independent review and appraisal of accounting, financial and other management systems. In the U.K. there is no statutory obligation for government departments to maintain an internal audit service but failure to do so may lead to criticism by the Public Accounts Committee (PAC). The permanent head of a government department is personally accountable to Parliament, through the PAC, for resources for which he or she is the Accounting Officer. Internal audit is seen as an important ally and source of advice.

The context for change

The prime responsibility of internal audit is to assure the Accounting Officer that the various internal control systems within the department are operating satisfactorily. In order to give this assurance, reviews are carried out, using a system-based approach to audit. This means that internal audit reviews and appraises the accounting financial and other controls relevant to the system under review. Internal audit should evaluate the controls established by management to:

- achieve their objectives;
- ensure the economical and efficient use of resources;
- ensure compliance with established policies, procedures, laws and regulations;
- safeguard their assets and interests from losses of all kinds, including those arising from fraud, irregularity or corruption;
- ensure the integrity and reliability of information and data.

As well as forming an opinion on the adequacy, reliability and effectiveness of the controls in each systems audited, the Head of Internal Audit (HIA) consolidates the results of the year's audits into an annual report in which is expressed an opinion on the whole system of internal control.

Internal audit also needs to consider and comment on, from the audit standpoint, new projects at their planning and development stages.

The HIA maintains an analysis of the organisation's systems and associated risks. This assessment forms the basis for producing short-term and longer range plans.

All systems within the audit universe will be risk assessed, their frequency of audit determined and the audit resource requirements calculated. Some high risk systems may require annual review while low risk systems are reviewed over a longer cycle. Normally the HIA will maintain a rolling programme of audits for a three- to five-year period, updating it annually. The annual plan, being the first slice, identifies the immediate audits to be performed and any other required audit activity.

Implementing change

The development of Internal Audit in the U.K. Government in its present form began in the early 1980s. In its report of 1981, the PAC criticised the general standard of internal audit in government departments and charged the Treasury to ensure that standards were raised. PAC's main concerns were:

- the audit of computer-based systems was inadequate;
- a lack of professional skill and management within audit;
- inadequate personnel policies;
- inadequate direction from the centre.

As a result departments were required to meet specified requirements in respect of staffing and work programmes of internal audit.

Key stakeholders were the PAC, National Audit Office and Treasury which thought that improving financial management in government could be assisted by the establishment of an effective internal audit service. The support of senior management in all government departments was also needed.

Potential obstacles may include the need to overcome negative management attitudes to audit, seeing it as a policeman rather than as an aid to management, and, once this resistance is overcome, the need to convince management, often working with restricted resources, that the benefits of an effective internal audit service, which may not be easily quantifiable, outweigh the costs.

Improvement in internal audit has been achieved through the following:

- the introduction of Standards for internal audit as set down in the Government Internal Audit Manual (GIAM). This was first published in 1983, revised in 1988 and is currently under review with the aim of a revised version to be published in 1994/95;

- introduction of a comprehensive training programme for Internal Auditors, designed to meet the Basic Audit Training Standard which is set out in GIAM;

- a programme of reviews by Treasury's Internal Audit Development Division (IADD) to ensure compliance with Standards, to identify areas for improvement, and to disseminate best practice.

Standards: The Internal Audit Development Branch of the Accountancy Finance and Audit Division had the role of setting internal audit standards and monitoring progress. IADD was established as a separate division of the Treasury in 1985. It has eight audit and three support staff and a budget of £340,000.

Training: An effective internal audit unit requires a mix of skills, not only professional skills which can be developed through training, but also personal skills, particularly the ability to communicate orally and in writing with staff at all levels. A training programme of 18 weeks' (now reduced to 14) formal tuition in various internal audit-related subjects was established, in conjunction with the Civil Service College and a number of institutes of Higher Education. Formal exams at the end of the course, combined with practical experience certified by the Head of Internal Audit, lead to the award of the Basic Audit Training Standard. Staff are also encouraged to obtain a professional qualification in internal audit, such as Membership of the Institute of Internal Auditors. This has led to the professionalisation of the U.K. Government internal audit service. The cost of training an internal auditor is about £14,000 excluding salary costs. A number of additional training courses, for example, for senior audit managers, or for computer audit specialists, are also available and internal audit staff are encouraged to take appropriate training.

The initial costs depend on whether a training programme is already available which can be easily adapted to government needs or whether one needs to be developed from scratch. Thereafter, the bulk of the costs will be recurrent staffing costs. In the U.K. trained internal auditors were in great demand by the private sector and there was considerable loss of staff. Internal auditors here are therefore paid higher salaries than those for some comparable Civil Service grades in order to retain staff.

Reviews: Since 1988, IADD has conducted a series of reviews of selected aspects of internal audit activities; this marks a change from the previous policy which was to review all aspects of internal audit in specific departments. About a dozen departments are selected for each review which covers a particular aspect of internal audit or the standards. The aim is to identify weaknesses in approach as well as good examples from which other units can learn. Each department reviewed receives a letter containing any detailed observations and an overall report is copied to all Principal Finance Officers (PFOs).

After about three reviews (approximately a year) the process is completed by the Head of the Government Accountancy Service and Chief Accountancy Adviser to the Treasury writing to Permanent Heads of Departments asking for confirmation that any necessary action has been taken. Examples of subjects have been reviewed are staffing, performance management, computer audit and fraud.

IADD is also a source of information and advice for internal audit units, organises two conferences a year on internal audit topics, and produces a quarterly magazine distributed to all government internal auditors.

Progress has been steady over the last ten years. In November 1987 the Tenth Report of the PAC was published. Its main conclusions were that:

a) improvements had been made but many units were still not achieving the standards laid down;

b) staffing shortages gave rise for concern about senior management's commitment to internal audit;

c) the staffing position in computer audit was worrying.

The standard of internal audit was, however, much improved compared to the early 1980s, and much progress has been made since then. The overall conclusion from IADD's programme of reviews has been that IAUs are well ordered with appropriate planning and approach. There are fewer vacancies and the proportion of qualified staff has improved though there are still concerns about the shortage of staff skilled in computer audit. New guidance on Information Systems Audit (Computer Audit) has been prepared and will shortly be issued.

The development and structure of internal audit in departments is now being affected by the proposed extension of market-testing to specialist and professional skills. Some internal audit units have already been market-tested. IADD has a role in advising departments on tendering and the establishment of specifications for audit services.

As a result of development of agencies and the moves towards market-testing, it has been necessary to reconsider elements of the GIAM standards to indicate more clearly which parts are mandatory and which are guidance on practice; the current revision will also incorporate any changes identified as necessary as a result of IADD's programme of reviews.

Supporting material

(i) The role of Internal Audit and the standards to which it works is set out in the Government Internal Audit Manual, available from HMSO. ISBN 0-11-560018-3, 1988, £13.00

(ii) The Government Information Systems Audit Manual (GISAM) HMSO, ISBN 0-11-560051-5, 1993, £20.00

6.2 External auditing

Most external auditing of U.K. public bodies is carried out by the National Audit Office (NAO), although some bodies are audited by private sector firms. Local Authorities and Health Authorities are audited by the Audit Commission (England and Wales) and the Scottish Accounts Commission (Scotland). There is a separate Northern Ireland Audit Office auditing public bodies in the Province. In the U.K., public sector external auditors are independent of Government and work directly to the Commissions or, as in NAO's case, to Parliament.

The National Audit Office is wholly independent of the Executive and Judiciary. Its work is governed by three Acts of Parliament:

- the Exchequer and Audit Departments Act 1866;
- the Exchequer and Audit Departments Act 1921; and
- the National Audit Act 1983.

The NAO is headed by the Comptroller and Auditor General (C & AG) who is appointed by the Queen, on the advice of the Prime Minister and the Chairman of the Public Accounts Committee (PAC). The independence and tenure of the C & AG is assured since removal from Office is the prerogative by the Queen following an address by both Houses of Parliament. The position is not fixed term and the salary is paid directly from the Consolidated Fund without requiring the annual approval of the Executive or of Parliament. The C & AG alone decides on the extent and conduct of the audits and other examinations carried out and the content of the reports he makes to Parliament.

The NAO's primary role is to provide independent assurance, information and advice to Parliament on the accounts of government departments and a wide range of other public bodies, and on the economy, efficiency and effectiveness with which they use their resources. This is done by certifying annual accounts and publishing independent reports on the results of value for money examination. It provides a similar service to the governing bodies of many international organisations.

Under the 1983 Act the C & AG was empowered to appoint such staff and determine their rates of pay as the postholder considers necessary to discharge the functions of the office. In doing so, the C & AG is expected to take account of the general rates of pay applicable to the Civil Service.

The 1983 Act also provides the statutory basis for NAO's reports on the results of both audits of accounts and examinations of the economy, efficiency and effectiveness with which audited bodies use their resources. The NAO publishes their value for money reports to meet their primary value for money aim of providing Parliament with independent assurance, information and advice on the use of major resources in departments and other audited bodies. They are written for the Parliamentary reader and for the public in general. The Act does not entitle NAO to question the merits of policy objectives.

National Audit Office reports are considered by the House of Commons Public Accounts Committee who have power to send for persons, papers and records and to make visits outside Parliament. It takes evidence in public from the Accounting Officer or Chief Executive of the department or body concerned. Other officials may attend and can also give evidence. C & AG and Treasury officials are also present. The PAC tends to concentrate on value for money reports. They make their own reports to the House, including appropriate recommendations for action by the government department concerned.

The Government's response to such recommendations is made in "Treasury Minutes" laid before the House. It is this process which gives real effect to findings in the C & AG reports. The Committee's work and the Government's response to it may also be debated by the whole House on one or two days a year. The NAO follow up recommendations made in Treasury Minutes and normally report to the PAC if there is a delay or lack of progress in implementing the recommendations.

NAO audits to standards which are consistent with best professional practice in the U.K. and international auditing environment. An audit follows a planned and thorough approach:

- gaining management awareness of the audited body's business and of its financial procedures;
- preparing an audit plan for approval at Directorate (i.e. partner) level;
- conducting audit tests and recording the results;
- management review of the audit results;
- audit completion, culminating in the Comptroller and Auditor General's opinion on the financial statements.

The context for change

In recent years, the U.K. Government has taken steps to improve the management of the massive resources devoted to running public services. One of the key aspects of both the Financial Management Initiative and the Next Steps Programme has been the drive to set clear objectives for managers and to introduce systems to measure output and performance. The Citizen's Charter has highlighted the importance of quality, choice, standards and value in public sector services.

External auditors, whilst naturally independent of government, have provided material for reports to Parliament on the implementation of these initiatives by:

- Providing audit opinions and reports on the financial statements of the organisations. This material considers regularity, propriety and stewardship and ensures that both Treasury direction and generally accepted accounting practice have been followed in the preparation of the financial statements;

- Examining the economy, efficiency and effectiveness of the organisations. This will consider how the initiatives themselves have been implemented, as well as the value for money actually delivered by the service;

- Providing advice and guidance to new agencies on accounting systems and policies and technical issues. For example, NAO is very often asked to comment on draft accounts directions for new bodies.

The overall objective is to ensure that the financial statements which they audit provide users, principally Members of Parliament, with relevant and reliable information. This information must be supported to give assurances that monies voted by Parliament have been used as intended and that budgets have not been exceeded. The information must be adequate to help them judge whether resources have been used efficiently and effectively.

Implementing change

Legislation provides an external audit body with its remit; independence from the executive; a source of funds and arrangements for oversight. In the U.K. the 1983 Act established a Public Accounts Commission with three main functions in respect of NAO:

- to appoint an accounting officer;
- to appoint an auditor, and
- to examine expenses incurred.

NAO employs about 800 staff including both professional and support grades. It recruits graduate trainees who are then required to qualify with the professional accounting institutes in the United Kingdom.

Experience has shown that the skills necessary for a successful audit team are essentially the same as would be required for any successful business venture: qualified accountants, accounting technicians, statisticians and computer specialists, backed up by good quality administration staff, including personnel, finance and building services specialists. It is important that the balance is correct between the various grades and skill levels of staff and this is particularly so in relation to audit grades. It is also important that, to attract the highest calibre staff, pay rates are consistent with the private sector and there are promotion and career development prospects.

It is necessary to buy-in specialist assistance from time to time on short-term contracts. The NAO does this particularly on value for money audits, where a topic is so specialised that skills from other professions are needed in order to consider properly all the issues. Examples include pharmacists, engineers, retired military officers etc. However, the practice is not restricted solely to VFM audit. Specialist assistance is contracted in when auditing financial statements, for example, in relation to the audit of pension schemes or charities or with regard to taxation matters.

Key stakeholders, in addition to those listed, include the support of a Parliamentary body to whom the auditors report (i.e. the PAC) and who guarantee the auditors' status and rights of access to information. A second Parliamentary body, The Public Accounts Commission (TPAC), oversees their operations, approves their funding and their strategic plans.

6.3 Accruals-based accounting, assessing value for money, and introducing capital charging

Improving the efficiency, output and outcome performance of the public sector in the U.K. has been a high priority for the Government over the last decade. A number of public sector management initiatives have been introduced:

- Financial Management Initiative (FMI), launched in 1982. This marked the start of a general and co-ordinated drive to improve financial management in government departments. One of the key aims was to devolve responsibility for budgets and financial control to line management units and to individuals wherever possible, giving them clear objectives and full information to help their decisions.

- The Multi-Departmental Review of Budgeting (MDRB) which in 1986 focused on the need for top management to set priorities, manage resources and review performance and for achievements to be evaluated regularly.

- The Government Purchasing Initiative (GPI) which in 1984 aimed to develop professionalism in Government Purchasing and to set up a unit to improve value for money through best practice.

- The Next Steps Initiative (1988), whose aim is to deliver government services more efficiently and effectively and devolve executive functions of government to agencies. Chief Executives of Agencies are directly and personally responsible to Ministers for their performance.

This entry deals with three topics relevant to the drive for greater efficiency:

i) the use of accruals-based accounting;

ii) assessing value for money;

iii) introducing capital charging.

Accruals-based accounting

In contrast to cash accounting, the accruals method records income (revenue) and expenditure (costs) as they are respectively earned and incurred, not as money is received and paid. For stewardship purposes, the transactions are brought together in an "income and expenditure account" covering the financial period. For example, a sale is recorded when a body has the right to demand payment from the customer, and a purchase is recorded when the liability to pay has arisen. In addition, the cost (or current value) of fixed assets is charged against income as depreciation over the estimated useful lives of the assets.

The advantages of accruals accounting are:

- Easier to measure financial performance, e.g. the extent to which costs are recovered and the percentage return being earned on capital employed. Financial targets are normally set in these terms;

- Establishes the resources consumed in a period (not cash disbursed) and accordingly provides a means of setting efficiency targets and measuring the actual performance achieved.

Budgeting and financial reporting for the "core" (non-commercial) elements of the U.K. public sector have traditionally been on a cash basis. Parliament votes an annual grant to departments on the basis of estimated payments and receipts within a year. This is then compared with actual payments and receipts at the end of each year.

In commercial parts of the public sector, accrual accounts along private sector lines have been the norm. Several departments engaged in manufacturing and trading have prepared their accounts on this basis for many years. However, of the traditional areas of government, only the Executive Agencies launched in 1988 have been expected to prepare commercial-style accruals accounts. Consideration is currently being given to extending similar arrangements to government departments.

The context for change

Following the introduction of accruals-based accounting in Agencies, attention is now turning to the traditional departments, where accounts are still prepared on a cash basis. However, the requirements for efficiency in resource allocation and value for money in service provision are just as important as in Agencies. Whilst cash accounting is still essential for the purpose of controlling cash, it is not the best way of judging value for money. There is no mechanism for dealing with depreciation of capital assets, interest on capital or internal charges within the cash budgeting system. It is against this background that the U.K. Treasury is introducing a pilot study on accrual accounting in a number of departments. This will consider:

- whether the new system is demonstrably useful to departments in terms of allocating resources and improving value for money;

- whether the cost of introducing the new system is reasonable;

- whether it will provide information to Select Committees, MPs, academics and the public in terms of enhancing accountability.

Public sector reform in the U.K., involving reduced detailed controls over managers, greater flexibility in resource use, making managers more accountable for performance within a clear framework of objectives and resources, and the underlying pre-eminent objective of producing value for money in public services, have clearly demonstrated the need for additional, more robust indicators of financial performance than traditional cash-based accounting arrangements can provide. New accrual-based financial reporting is seen as an adjunct to traditional cash reporting (not a replacement for it), which will enhance the tools available to assess and reflect performance in value for money terms.

The introduction of delegated budgetary responsibility and executive agencies called for refinement of existing accounting arrangements and development of new financial management procedures. The traditional system excluded from managers' control a number of non-cash resource items (e.g. depreciation, cost of capital, debtors, creditors, stock balances, rents, superannuation etc.) which were considered relevant, to varying degrees, to achievement of the broader results-orientated goals set for managers under various reform initiatives. The focus, and assessment of performance, on the basis of value for money (VFM) criteria implied the need for financial management information which showed how total resources were applied and managed, in addition to information on cash payments and receipts.

The creation of Executive Agencies contains the main structural shift in recognition of the need for accruals-based data as a means for managers to plan, address and be accountable for, performance in value for money terms. It has also provided additional means for Parliament and users of public services more objectively to assess public sector performance.

The presumption is that accruals accounting will bring real benefits to Agency management. Assessment of the system will be a main feature in initial reviews of individual Agency framework documents.

Implementing change

U.K. experience suggests that the following are among the basic requirements or preconditions for successful introduction of accruals-based accounting:

i) non-cash items to be brought into the cash accounting system, for example, opportunity cost rentals and superannuation;

ii) supplementary accruals-based information to be produced – memorandum trading accounts and capital asset registers;

iii) additional requirements calling for accrual-based, rather than cash-based, information need to be made as a result of market testing and for Executive Agencies.

There needs to be continuous involvement of professional accountants and senior management, and professional accountancy staff in the department need to be committed to the change. There is often difficulty in obtaining agreement to introduce accrual accounts from those whom the old system has served well.

Starting from scratch, the whole exercise is likely to take a minimum of two years. This could be shorter if elements of the required system are already in place, e.g. if the body has already been operating a chargeable service based on full cost recovery, using memorandum accounts; or longer if the body has a large number of outlets widely spaced across the country and supplies a large range of goods and services.

The typical steps or stages in implementing accruals accounting are as follows:

i) set up a Steering Group and a Project Team with responsibility for the task;

ii) recruit the necessary expertise, if not available in-house;

iii) determine the data to be captured:

- fixed assets and investments
- raw materials, stocks and work in progress
- debtors and creditors
- pre-payments and accrued income
- provisions
- capital and reserves
- turnover and other income
- cost of sales
- operating expenses;

iv) determine the type and frequency of the management and financial information required;

v) decide the accounting policies;

vi) draw up a system specification and implementation plan, including the required go-live date;

vii) select consultants, if necessary (likely to be needed, unless the in-house team is highly competent and has adequate resources);

viii) select the hardware and software required to operate the system;

ix) set up the necessary accounting code structure;

x) install the selected system, and adapt as necessary (keeping adaptations to a minimum);

xi) test run the system;

xii) confirm, or amend, the date for live running.

In November 1993 the Chancellor of the Exchequer announced a decision in principle that government departments should introduce resource accounting systems based on commercial accounting principles similar to those already in place in Agencies and most other parts of the public sector. Detailed proposals were set out in a Green Paper on Resource Accounting and Budgeting, published in July 1994. The introduction of resource accounting will help departments to manage their current and capital resources more efficiently and effectively and to relate the cost of their inputs more closely to their objectives and outputs.

Assessing value for money (VFM)
This frequently arises in an auditing context (internal and external), but can equally receive priority within an organisation's normal management structure. Many U.K. Government organisations tackle it through:

- initial appraisal of capital projects;
- post-contract reviews of projects;
- special reviews of services, whole units of government, or programmes of expenditure.

The VFM dimension runs through U.K. structures in other ways. For instance, in the criteria used to decide whether it is better to provide something in-house or buy it from the wider marketplace. VFM requires a consideration of "life-cycle" costs, e.g. the ongoing cost of maintenance throughout the expected life of buildings and equipment.

Introducing capital charging
In the U.K. Government, this operates at two levels:

i) The general externally imposed rule that departmental trading units and Agencies must include in their costs (on which their performance is partly based) interest on capital at a rate fixed by the Treasury. This is part of working to a "full economic cost" (FEC) base.

ii) Within Agencies of central government and certainly within the National Health Service and latterly local government in the U.K., interest is normally charged within the management (internal) accounts to impress upon local managers the real costs of the assets they hold and thereby encourage efficient use of them.

Usually, the greatest difficulty arises in the initial stage of defining the assets utilised (capital and current) by each accountable unit within the organisation. Obviously, this is much easier if accrual accounting has been in operation for some time, in the establishment of reliable asset registers, generally computer-based.

Suporting material

Better Accounting for the Taxpayer's Money: Resource Accounting and Budgeting in Government, HMSO, Cm 2626, £9.40

6.4 Estate management

This paper covers developments since 1983 in the management of the Civil Estate – as distinct from the Defence Estate or other Operational Estates (e.g. Prisons) – and explains the role of Property Holdings (PH) since 1990 as central manager of the Common User Estate (CUE). The aims of PH are:

- to work with other government departments in managing the CUE in such a way as to meet their accommodation requirements economically, effectively and efficiently;
- to recover from departments the full cost of their accommodation on the CUE and also to collect opportunity cost rents on the Departmental Estate (specialised properties managed directly by the departments occupying them); and
- in all aspects of its work, to act as an environmentally aware organisation.

Originally, the Government's Estate was managed centrally and accommodation was simply made available to departments as necessary. There were no arrangements for charging individual departments for the accommodation they occupied.

In 1983, the Property Repayment System (PRS) was introduced. At first this was a broad cost signal and then it was progressively refined (1984-88) and there was a gradual increase in the works delegation to occupying departments.

In 1990, the Civil Estate was divided. Property Holdings was then set up to manage the "Common User" estate, mainly general purpose offices comprising about 72 million square feet in approximately 3,000 properties, with the remaining 40% of the Government's former Civil Estate, mostly specialised and storage buildings like courts and laboratories, or buildings in remote locations, managed from then by individual occupying departments.

On the Common User Estate, departments became responsible and accountable for deciding the amount, location and quality of accommodation they required and then paying for it. Property Holdings were responsible for identifying and advising on the range of options and costs for meeting departments' office requirements. PH was responsible for managing the CUE portfolio as a common resource across departments, so as to be able to offer departments accommodation which represented best value for money. Departments are tied to using PH for specific services which are essential to PH's strategic management role which need to be carried out centrally.

The context for change

The Financial Management Initiative in 1982 resulted in managers having:

- clear objectives;
- resource budgets to implement;
- being subject to critical scrutiny of the output and value for money of resources employed.

Accommodation is one of the key resources employed, and with the emphasis placed on resource management, many departments sought more direct control over their accommodation.

With departments responsible for the cost of their own accommodation, stewardship of resources is likely to be more thorough and better value for money should be achieved.

Implementing change

The U.K. experience has shown that the basic requirements or pre-conditions for successful action in this field are charging, organisation and structure and liaison which is in turn dependent on departments being organised themselves to deal with accommodation matters.

The skills necessary to achieve these results include professional advice, accounting and general management and communication skills.

Key stakeholders, whose commitment is necessary for success are the Treasury, larger departments and parent department.

In the U.K.'s experience, the obstacles to achieving success are likely to be the capital programme, fluctuations in the market and sudden changes in requirements/unforeseen accommodation demands.

The Government announced in May 1988 that the Common User element of the Civil Estate was to be managed by Property Holdings, and specialised properties would become the responsibility of individual occupying departments. The division took effect from 1 April 1990.

6.5 Improving procurement and purchasing procedures

Procurement is the overall process of acquiring goods and services to meet customer needs. The procurement cycle begins when a need is identified, and ends when the required goods or services have been paid for. But the procurement process goes beyond the cycle to cover more strategic issues such as procurement strategy, storage, distribution/logistics and external resource (supplier) management. Procurement is synonymous with 'total supply chain management'. Purchasing is a subset of the procurement cycle and involves activities such as sourcing, negotiating and contracting for goods or services.

In January 1986, the Treasury's Central Unit on Purchasing (CUP) was created to take forward the Government Purchasing Initiative. CUP's role is to offer help and advice to central government departments and agencies on best purchasing practice and achieving better value for money (VFM) in purchasing and supply. It also monitors departments' progress in implementing the recommendations in the 1984 Report "Government Purchasing". Since 1986, its role has been extended to providing advice and guidance to departments on the commercial aspects of market testing activities and project management in the works/construction field. The Unit is staffed with a mix of civil servants and professional advisers on secondment from the private sector.

The context for change

The Central Unit on Purchasing was established to address a number of areas of concern, identified in the 1984 Report, for example:

- concern that the Government were not getting best value for money from its significant spend on goods and services;
- lack of professionalism among staff engaged in purchasing;
- inadequate training and career development programmes for purchasing staff;
- inadequate exposure to commercial experience and "state of the art" techniques;
- insufficient awareness of cost and time-saving techniques;
- inadequate information systems to support the development of purchasing strategy.

Both *market-testing* and *competitive tendering* are closely linked to procurement.

Market-testing is a management initiative which aims to ensure that services are delivered which provide best value for money for the taxpayer. The development of market testing programmes is essentially a management task, although there may be input from procurement professionals at the planning stage (for example, advice on conditions in the market and the availability of potential, external contractors to undertake the work – which may influence the choice of services to be tested).

To secure best value for money, *competitive tendering* exercises are run which ascertain the overall cost of either providing the service in-house, or contracting it out to a third party supplier. This process is essentially a procurement exercise. However, buying services is intrinsically more difficult than buying goods, and requires special skills in the staff involved. The keys to success are having a clear, performance-based specification of the services required, allowing potential suppliers to offer innovative solutions, and developing contracts which provide incentives for improved performance by the supplier.

Implementing change

Experience in the U.K. suggests that the essential pre-requisites for developing purchasing practice include the following:

Costs

- knowing how much is being spent, on which goods and services and with which suppliers;

- knowing who is spending the money within the organisation.

Skills

- equipping staff engaged in purchasing with the requisite skills through formal training and career development programmes.

Key stakeholders

- budget-holders: convincing them that purchasing is important and that value for money opportunities do exist.

Information

- essential for the development of purchasing strategy – to identify where the major opportunities exist;

- giving purchasing staff relevant up-to-date guidance on best practice and techniques;

- visibility – encouraging departments to set challenging targets for value for money improvement, monitoring progress and publishing performance.

CUP has an advisory role and does not prescribe to individual departments and agencies. Their progress has been variable across U.K. Government. But U.K. experience suggests the following broad timescales:

- publication of original proposals to establishing the Central Unit on Purchasing: one year;

- creating a professional cadre of purchasing staff with the requisite skills: at least five years;

- the development and implementation of integrated procurement systems: three to five years.

A recent study of the organisation of procurement has identified seven key success factors which characterise effective and successful procurement activity:

i) a clear policy and strategy for developing procurement activity;

ii) effective management information and control systems;

iii) development of procurement expertise and its deployment;

iv) a procurement role in corporate management;

v) an entrepreneurial, pro-active approach towards its role in the organisation, working in partnership with users;

vi) focus resources and efforts on those areas where they will be of most value;

vii) central co-ordination of procurement activities to ensure sharing of expertise, efficiency and VFM, through aggregation of demand and rationalisation of products or suppliers.

This sets the basic agenda for CUP's future activities.

As part of the general drive to ensure that civil servants are equipped with the skills experience and capabilities they need, 45 per cent of purchasers in key government posts are currently working towards professional qualifications. The target is to have that increased to 75 per cent by 1996.

Supporting material

Government Purchasing, Progress Report to the Prime Minister, HMSO 1992, ISBN 0 11 560047 7, £22.00

6.6 End year flexibility

This entry covers both capital and running costs expenditure of central government. In principle, money voted for one specific year has had to be spent during that year. If it is not spent, it has traditionally been forfeited. The purpose of end year flexibility (EYF) is to avoid or minimise this restriction.

The context for change

The objectives of the end year flexibility scheme are:

- to avoid potential disruption arising from unavoidable slippage from one year to the next;
- to reduce surges of spending at the year end, which have poor value for money and are often wasteful.

Implementing change

In 1983, departments were allowed to carry forward into the next financial year any underspending on eligible *capital* expenditure. Departments are encouraged to delegate EYF carry over to individual line or project management level, to enable project managers to secure the proper management benefits from the scheme.

The scheme allows up to five per cent of cash-limited eligible provision (voted or non-voted) to be carried forward from one year to the next. But the rules ensure that capital underspend must first be used to cover any overspend on other parts of a cash limit. Rollover to a further year is possible, but the maximum entitlement in a year is limited to five per cent of the sum of the capital provision for the previous year and entitlement not taken up (or £2 million if greater).

Entitlements are announced by the Chief Secretary in an arranged Parliamentary Question each July on the basis of figures in the annual White Paper on the provisional out-turn for cash limits in the previous year. Parliamentary rules on annual authorisation for voted expenditure still apply, since in that case the money has to be re-voted in a Supplementary Estimate. Increases in provision resulting from the take-up of end year flexibility are charged to the Reserve.

The *running costs* scheme, introduced in 1988, is likewise intended to help departmental management and budgeting. It is available to departments operating under the gross running costs control regime who have:

i) secured in the Survey a three-year settlement for their running costs provision, based on a satisfactory management plan. Nearly all major departments now have three-year survey settlements;

ii) satisfied the Treasury that they can operate an EYF scheme on running costs in a way that will continue to improve efficiency.

Carry-over was originally limited to one half per cent of the year's final running cost limit but, following a recent review, the EYF for 1993-94 carry-over is now unlimited. As with the capital scheme, underspending must first be used to offset any excesses elsewhere on a Vote. The position on entitlements and take-up is similar to that for the capital scheme.

The carry-forward of underspends from one year to the next results in higher public expenditure than would otherwise have been the case if the carry-forward had remained an underspend. There is also the hidden cost of the uncertainty which carry-forward has on forecasting public expenditure. By the very nature of the scheme, the eligible underspends cannot be identified until the end of the financial year and their levels can vary substantially from year to year. There are also administrative costs associated with the schemes.

The key stakeholders are the project managers. One of the main objectives of the scheme is to avoid low-value end year spending. If a department centrally retained the EYF facility for overall cash management purposes, the incentive for individuals at project management level to avoid underspends would continue.

SECTION 7: IMPROVING POLICY-MAKING

7.1 Enhancing policy analysis

7.2 Enhancing policy co-ordination

7.3 Improving policy presentation

7.1 Enhancing policy analysis

Policy analysis, evaluation and appraisal are closely inter-linked. Policy evaluation is the process of examining a policy while it is in operation or after it has come to an end. It follows naturally from the policy appraisal which is the term normally used for an analysis done before a policy is launched. The techniques are similar. Appraisal helps to improve decision-making by considering whether a proposed policy is likely to be worthwhile and by comparing in advance the different options for putting it into practice. Evaluation enables the decisions taken as a result of the appraisal to be reviewed afterwards with the same rigour in the light of what has actually happened and with the knowledge of any changes in the external environment which may have occurred in the meantime. It is important that policies should be properly analysed and evaluated to ensure that they are achieving their purpose and giving value for money.

Evaluation helps policy managers to achieve their objectives. It can be seen as part of a policy-making cycle which begins with appraisal; leads on through identification of options to decisions; and is then followed by implementation, monitoring and evaluation, back to reappraisal. To the extent that evaluation considers what might have happened if other policies had been adopted, it is merging into reappraisal. Evaluation is to be distinguished from monitoring, that is routine checking of progress against plan, although monitoring will often contribute much useful information and is itself an essential part of the process. Evaluation requires a critical and detached look both at the objectives and how they are being met.

The context for change

Policy evaluation and analysis are not new, but are being given greater emphasis and more systematic attention within the U.K. Government as part of the Financial Management Initiative and the drive to improve Civil Service management and accountability generally. They form one aspect of a broad stream of management changes introduced in recent years.

Implementing change

There are differences in practice among departments concerning responsibility for commissioning and undertaking evaluations – the line manager, a central unit, or some combination of the two, with or without help from outside experts such as consultants. HM Treasury take the lead in co-ordinating the general approach to policy analysis and have issued a detailed Guide for Managers which sets out the basic essentials.

Various strategies have been employed to improve management across government. One approach has been a formal requirement to deliver certain services or activities to a specified standard, e.g. accounts directives from the Treasury or the Cabinet paper rules on policy evaluation). Considerable pressure to improve management has been brought about through the Public Expenditure Survey, and through various central initiatives under the "Financial Management" umbrella. The emphasis on the development of output and performance measurements; and the shift to greater delegation to departments in areas such as financial systems and control, pay and personnel matters are examples of this trend.

Cabinet Office instructions on papers for submission to Cabinet say that all proposed policy changes should "make clear what is to be achieved, by when, and at what cost, and how this achievement is to be measured". Departments are also required, where there are public expenditure implications, to clear these with the Treasury before submitting to Cabinet.

There is little available information about how successfully departments have been applying those instructions or guidance, but the picture seems rather patchy. There are examples of errors in the approach between the policy development and appraisal (e.g. too few options examined, unjustified optimism in determining key assumptions, or failure to take account of behavioural effects).

Some departments have developed extensive systems of policy evaluation but others have made less progress since the guidance was launched five years ago, and the returns in the most recent survey were somewhat disappointing. Evaluation has been very difficult where the appraisal stage was poorly prepared, and clear objectives for policies and profiles of costs and outcome were not constructed at the outset.

There is no requirement for departments to report to a central body such as the Treasury or Cabinet Office, or to Parliament on the evaluation of their policies. Departments may use their departmental reports as a vehicle, but in practice few have chosen to do so.

Recent developments reinforce the importance of policy evaluation work:

- the top-down approach in the Public Expenditure Survey;
- the more strategic relationship between Treasury and departments;
- fundamental reviews of programme expenditure.

The "Top-Down" Survey: In recent years the approach adopted in the Public Expenditure Survey has been to establish an overall base line within which individual programmes are constrained. Against this background, Ministers have to make balanced choices between programmes both at inter-departmental and intra-departmental level. These choices should be informed by thorough analysis of the effectiveness of existing programmes.

The speed with which the centre moves to a more ***strategic relationship*** with departments will to some extent depend on how successful departments are in delivering their policy aims and objectives. This is turn needs the support of a wide range of project and policy appraisals/evaluations, fully covering each department's business.

The Chief Secretary to the Treasury has launched a comprehensive series of ***fundamental reviews*** of programme expenditure. This year they are being undertaken in four departments and, although these are at the strategic level, they will need to be underpinned by relevant project/policy appraisals and evaluations.

In view of the increasing importance of policy analysis, it is clear that further development of techniques and identification of obstacles is desirable if progress is to be made.

Supporting material

(i) "Policy Evaluation – A Guide for Managers", HM Treasury, HMSO 1988, ISBN 0-11-560015-9, £3.50

(ii) "Economic Appraisal in Central Government: A Technical Guide for Government Departments", HM Treasury, HMSO 1991 ISBN 0-11-560034-5, £7.50

7.2 Enhancing policy co-ordination

This entry is based on the functions of the U.K. Cabinet Office, which is not a policy department, but which is instrumental in co-ordinating policy across government through the Cabinet Committee system.

The Cabinet Office serves both Cabinet and the network of Cabinet Committees which jointly consider and endorse government policies. It is a long established system designed to ensure that all policies are carefully examined for possible cross-departmental implications (including public expenditure indications). Committee membership is drawn from a wide range of departments, including all those with a direct interest in the area of policy in question.

Departments with significant policy initiatives are required to clear them through the appropriate Committee. In most cases, this can be done through correspondence. The Minister concerned writes to the Chairman of the appropriate Committee with copies to members and the Cabinet Secretariat. Members respond, giving their views. When all members have either commented or indicated that they are content, the Chairman writes to the originating Minister and signifies the approval of the Committee to the policy, subject to the points made.

Where a subject is of major importance it may be considered at a meeting of the Committee. In this case, the Minister seeking approval circulates a Memorandum to the Committee which is then discussed. The Chairman sums up the discussion, and either signifies the Committee's approval or suggests further work which needs to be done. Subjects of very great importance may need to be decided by Cabinet itself. In all cases, the Secretariat support is provided by the Cabinet Office. There is also a network of official Committees serviced by the Cabinet Office, dealing with the day-to-day cross-departmental co-ordination of policy.

Once policies have been approved, their translation into legislation is also subject to a procedure involving two special Cabinet Committees (the Ministerial Committees on Legislation (LG) and on the Queen's Speeches and Future Legislation (FLG)). Bids for Bills are sought annually from departments and a Legislative Programme is recommended to Cabinet by FLG Committee. Once approval has been given to a Bill, it is drafted and examined by LG Committee before it is introduced into Parliament. LG is not a policy Committee, but ensures that all the necessary policy approvals have been given to the provisions of the Bill as drafted, before agreeing to its introduction.

7.3 Improving policy presentation

Putting over the message of government policy falls primarily into two categories:

- paid publicity (e.g. through advertising campaigns);
- press and information service (responding to the media and supplying them with news and information).

Each department has its own objectives but generally those of its information division will be:

- to create and maintain an informed opinion about the subjects with which each department deals;
- to use all the methods of publicity where suitable to help the department achieve its purpose;
- to help and advise in all matters bearing on relations between the department and its public; and
- to advise the department of the public's reaction to the policies or actions of the department.

Governments have a duty to inform the public concerning the introduction of new legislation, its impact, and what their duties and responsibilities are.

Government decisions fall broadly into two categories – those that require legislation and those that do not. In both instances, a department's information staff have a role to play in the presentation of information. Sometimes, simply reporting and building on newsworthy policy introductions will achieve the desired result but on other occasions paid publicity is necessary to reinforce and get home the message.

Experience in the U.K. Civil Service suggests that it is essential for the information staff to be consulted from the first moment that the policy begins to take shape. They will then be able to comment on the draft announcement, advise on methods of presentation and likely public reaction. It will be important for them to plan well ahead with advertising budgets, selection of media, media availability etc. in good time.

The method of presentation is decided upon once the policy is clear. Depending on the significance of the announcement, this can include a mix of:

- press notice;
- press briefing;
- press conference;
- ministerial interviews;
- ministerial articles;
- photo call;
- press facility to inspect new installation/equipment/project;
- paid publicity campaign (press/radio/TV advertisements, publicity leaflets, point of sale material, exhibitions, videos, advertising gifts and handouts etc.).

Experience suggests that the first presentation of government policy is vital, but in the weeks following the launch of a policy, ill-informed criticism can often begin to affect public attitudes. The information officer must be prepared to suggest follow-up action. This can take many forms. It may be that a journalist can be persuaded to write a well-informed article dealing with the criticism, perhaps after a briefing by the Minister. It might be necessary to issue a correction or the Minister may wish to give a TV or radio news interview to answer critics and to put the record straight. Letters to newspapers are not usually the best method of answering criticism, since they usually provoke further criticism. Articles by Ministers can be a useful way of informing the public, particularly if an article can be published to coincide with the launch of the policy, but it should be used sparingly.

Training for Press Officers or publicity teams is available from the Central Office of Information, whose courses are open to officers from other countries.

Press Officers seek to build good relationships with the media to generate an atmosphere of trust and co-operation, whilst understanding that this is not always possible. Regional outlets are cultivated, as well as national ones.

The Press Office provides an intelligence service to Ministers and the department on what is in the newspapers and broadcast media, and an early warning system of which stories may be forthcoming.

A broad checklist for assessing the strength of a departmental Press Office facility is as follows:

- professional information staff (essential skills – rapport, political finesse, reasoning, ability to work under pressure, creativity);

- accommodation should comprise a studio, where interviews can be recorded, and a separate room for press conferences;

- good, open internal communication channels;

- close proximity to Ministers;

- ready access to departmental information, the administrators and Ministers;

- staff need quickly to develop familiarity with all the national and major regional media outlets (broadcast and press);

- staff need to establish good working relationships with the media, administrators and Ministers;

- comprehensive distribution lists should be established for the national and regional media and the technical press for the issue of press notices;

- staff should provide a 24-hour press office service (normally an allocated press officer would be on call at home overnight and at weekends);

- systems to monitor news output (both broadcast and press) should be established;

- the Press Office should become firmly locked into the workings of the department (e.g. copied in on all policy documents produced by officials and invited to all policy-making meetings);

- clerical staff support team;

- communication system – adequate telephone system, word processing, photocopier, fax machine, stocks of headed note-paper for press releases, facility to receive output from news agency (e.g. Reuters or Associated Press etc.), TV, radio, daily receipt of all national newspapers and, ideally, the means of issuing press notices electronically.

Ordering HMSO publications

All HMSO publications referred to in the text can be obtained from the local HMSO stockist or from:

HMSO Publications Centre
PO Box 276
London SW8 5DT
UK

Telephone enquiries:	0171 873 0011
Telephone orders:	0171 873 9090
Facsimile orders:	0171 873 8200

Further publications from the Management and Training Services Division

Capacity Building for Management of Privatisation
Report of the regional consultation workshopmic Management and Planning
Case studies of selected Commonwealth countries
held at ZIPAM, Zimbabwe, March 1994

Economic Management and Planning
Case studies of selected Commonwealth countries
Bakul H Dholakia and Ravindra H Dholakia, 1994
price £7.95

Administrative and Managerial Reform in Government: a Commonwealth Portfolio of Good Practice
Proceedings of a pan-Commonwealth Working Group Meeting held in Kuala Lumpur, April 1993

Choices in Decentralisation
An overview and curriculum for central government officials responsible for the reorganisation of administration at the local level
Brian Smith, 1993

Government Information Technology Policies and Systems
Success strategies in developed and developing countries
Chun Kwong Han and Geoff Walsham, 1993

Information Technology Policies and Applications in the Commonwealth Developing Countries
Mayuri Odedra and Shirin Madon, edited by G Harindranath and Jonathan Liebenau, 1993
price £8.00

The Changing Role of Government: Administrative Structures and Reforms
Proceedings of a Commonwealth Roundtable held in Sydney, February 1992

Public Administration in Small Island States
edited by Randall Baker, 1992

Successful Decentralisation
Proceedings of a Roundtable held in Male, December 1992

The following publications will be available shortly from the Management Training Services Division:

Management of the Privatisation Process: a guide to policy-making and implementation
This topical publication provides a practical guide for policy-makers and enterprise managers involved in privatisation programmes

Performance Contracts: A Handbook for Practitioners
This handbook provides detailed information on the planning and implementation of performance contracts and includes selected cases from Commonwealth and non-Commonwealth countries

Other forthcoming publications include:

Organisational structure in the public sector: choosing options for change

Cabinet profiles of selected Commonwealth countries

These and many other publications of practical value to managers, administrators, advanced students and academics requiring in-depth insights into the trends and opportunities confronting government are available from:

Commonwealth Secretariat Publications
Marlborough House
Pall Mall
London SW1Y 5HX

Telephone: 0171 839 3411
Facsimile: 0171 930 0827